HEIRLOOM
LOVE

HEIRLOOM LOVE

Authentic Christianity for This Age of Persecution

DOMINIC SPUTO
with BRIAN SMITH

Unless otherwise indicated, all Scripture quotations are taken from the *Holy Bible,* NEW INTERNATIONAL VERSION, copyright © 1973, 1978, 1984 International Bible Society. Used by permission of Zondervan Bible Publishers.

Scripture quotations designated "NIV-2011" are taken from *The Holy Bible, New International Version* (NIV) ©1973, 1978, 1984, 2011 by Biblica, Inc.™ Used by permission. All rights reserved worldwide.

Scripture quotations designated "NASB" are taken from the *New American Standard Bible,* © 1960, 1962, 1963, 1968, 1971, 1972, 1973, 1975, 1977, by the Lockman Foundation, LaHabra California. Used by permission.

Scripture quotations designated "NLT" are taken from the *Holy Bible, New Living Translation,* copyright © 1996. Used by permission of Tyndale House Publishers, Inc., Wheaton, Illinois 60189. All rights reserved.

Scripture quotations designated "ESV" are taken from *English Standard Version.* Copyright © 2001 by Crossway Books/Good News Publishers, Wheaton, IL, tel: 630/682–4300, www.goodnews-crossway.org.

Scripture quotations designated "NKJV" are taken from *The New King James Version.* Copyright © 1982, Thomas Nelson, Inc. All rights reserved. Bible text from The New King James Version is not to be reproduced in copies or otherwise by any means except as permitted in writing by Thomas Nelson, Inc., 501 Nelson Place, Nashville, Tennessee, 37214–1000.

Italics in Scripture quotations have been added by the author for emphasis.

ISBN 978-0-9907911-2-6

For more information visit *www.MuteNoMore.com.*

Printed in Canada

Contents

PART III
LOVE REVIVED

PART I

LOVE LOST

I hold this against you:
You have forsaken your first love.

—Jesus to the Ephesian church, Revelation 2:4

CHAPTER 1

Tasteless Tomatoes, Lackluster Love

We can learn a lot about love from tomatoes.

Maybe I'd better explain. Go back with me two generations.

My grandparents were born and raised in Italy. They entered the US through Ellis Island and settled in New York City. I have a lot of great memories of them. They never learned English. My grandfather made his own wine by stomping grapes in his apartment bathtub. My fondest memory, although intimidating at the time, was of my grandmother right in my face, pinching my cheek and saying in a loud, threatening voice, *"Mangia."* Which I interpreted to mean, "Eat, or else." I affectionately blame her for my adult propensity for overeating.

With this background, I became a foodie before it was trendy. I grew up a foodie just because that's what Italians do: We take food to heart. That's how we share the love. And we shared a lot of love.

When my parents married, they moved from the city to Long Island. My mother's first priority in suburbia was to plant a garden and grow tomatoes.

In order to understand my mother's priorities, you have to know that although we ate great Italian food every day, the Sunday meal was always the family gem, the crowning culinary achievement to which we always looked forward. It was also typically our simplest meal. And it was always the same—pasta with homemade tomato sauce. Every Sunday, without exception. My mother's Sunday sauce recipe had been handed down through the generations; it was beyond compare.

The secret to my mother's Sunday sauce was, as you may have guessed, the tomatoes. My mother's tomatoes were irresistible. We couldn't wait to eat them. We used to take a salt shaker out to her garden and eat them right off the vine. My mother's home-grown strain were very different from the tomatoes you find in today's grocery stores.

You see, in an effort to come up with the perfect tomato, the agricultural industry has modified God's design for the fruit. They have selectively bred tomatoes for several desirable traits—especially redness (the original stock come in a variety of colors), roundness (versus innumerable odd and even ugly shapes), and firmer texture for durability during transportation and handling. Thanks to science, we now have great looking tomatoes in our markets. Unfortunately, somewhere along the way they lost the *flavor*. The engineered varieties taste bland and indistinct in comparison to their ancestors. Fortunately for the taste buds of humanity, some of the older, truly flavorful strains have been preserved. These are known as heirloom tomatoes, and if you've never tasted one, you literally don't know what you're missing. If you've grown up eating only the most recent strains—whether store-bought or home-grown—you have no idea how good God's tomatoes should taste. Tomatoes didn't lose their flavor overnight. Because the changes were introduced gradually over many years, even I, who experienced the real deal as a child, was fooled and didn't realize that they had lost their flavor until recently when I tasted an heirloom tomato for the first time in many years.

LOVE LIKE TOMATOES

The love practiced by many American Christians seems to have fallen to a fate similar to that of tomatoes. Some say that we've modified God's design, that the fruit has lost its irresistible flavor. Has our Christian love become bland and indistinct in comparison to that of our early church ancestors? Have we lost the distinctive savory essence that Jesus said would cause all men to know that He is the Son of God and that we are His disciples? (See John 13:34–35; also 17:21–23.) For those who answer yes to these questions, there is hope.

Fortunately, the seeds of heirloom love have been preserved in the Scriptures. Today we can regrow and produce authentic love by learning it from God's Word. If you have never tasted heirloom love, you truly don't know what you're missing. If you've tasted only twenty-first-century Western love, you have no idea how good God's design for Christian love should taste. Until you taste heirloom love, you can't appreciate God's world-winning flavor. It's literally out of this world. The original love strain was irresistible. It was so flavorful that people were coming to Christ even during times of intense persecution. They were willing to follow Jesus even if it meant losing their loved ones, their livelihoods and their very lives. In comparison, today we go to great lengths to woo people into the front door of a church, but in many cases there are just as many or more walking out the back door. Could it be that the seekers don't taste and see something worth living for—let alone dying for? Might the problem be rooted in our love?

Jesus foresaw and earnestly warned against tasteless Christianity:

> You are the salt of the earth. But if the salt loses its saltiness, how can it be made salty again? It is no longer good for anything, except to be thrown out and trampled by men. (Matthew 5:13)

Yet less than a century later some Christians had begun to exercise flavorless "love." When Jesus confronted the Ephesian church, He said that they had forsaken their first love. Even though the Ephesians were known for good works, for perseverance and for hating evil, Jesus was primarily concerned with their lapsed love, and He sternly warned them (and us) to return to it (Revelation 2:1–7).

And nearly two thousand years later, a similar strain of man-engineered "love" has taken root in American Christianity. We think we know love, but when we read the New Testament carefully and honestly, we discover that today's "love" is very different from the early church love that changed the world. We are familiar with the New Testament passages on love, but we seem to have lost the Lord's intended meaning and the application practiced by the first believers. We must return to the original seed. This book is about restoring heirloom love. The love that Jesus and His apostles taught, the love that the thriving early church practiced eagerly and passionately.

Seemingly few Western Christians today are familiar with the taste of heirloom love. It's time to reconsider what Jesus meant when He uttered His "new command":

Love one another. As I have loved you, so you must love one another. By this all men will know that you are my disciples, if you love one another. (John 13:34–35)

These days my family doesn't enjoy pasta with sauce every Sunday, but when we do it's exciting and we all look forward to it with eager anticipation. But even then, we make it with canned, tasteless tomatoes. If we want the authentic original, like that which my mother used to make, we have to start by growing our own tomatoes from heirloom seeds. Then I can say to my own children, "Taste this and see what you've been missing."

I invite every reader to taste heirloom love. Return with me to the early church in Scripture—to the teachings on love and to the people whose stories exemplify authentic love. Be prepared to challenge your assumptions about love.

What have we been missing?

CHAPTER 2

Tasting Authentic New Testament Christianity

A few years ago the Lord disciplined me with an incurable disease, and I literally wasted away to the point of death. In short, I was unfaithful with a large amount of money that the Lord had entrusted to me when a technology company that I started with two friends merged with another company and went public on NASDAQ. The status of money and the material things had lured my heart away from the Lord, and it almost cost me my life.

As I prepared to die, I was forced to acknowledge the worthlessness of this world's attractions when compared to treasure of lasting value. And since that was actually the Lord's purpose for my illness, He miraculously healed me. He then impressed upon me the need to write a stewardship plan for my life. So I sat down at my desk with pen and paper and prayed, "Lord, to whom should I give?"

The Lord answered by impressing upon me the question, "What does My Word say about it?"

I discovered that I didn't really have an answer beyond my general impressions and traditional American Christian teachings. So I spent the next several months studying what the Bible says about money and giving.

In my search for truth, I counted 545 verses in the New Testament that directly pertain to money and giving (see Appendix A). Of these verses, 119 deal with general stewardship principles and do not discuss specific purposes for giving. The remaining 426 verses do reveal God's purposes for our giving, and the resulting list of purposes is surprisingly simple. It includes only three categories of beneficiaries for biblical giving:

- 281 verses (66 percent) are specifically related to financially supporting poor, suffering and persecuted Christians—that is, our brothers and sisters in the Lord, not "the needy" in general.[1]

- 88 verses (21 percent) pertain to financially supporting "the poor" without distinction between Christians and non-Christians.

- 57 verses (13 percent) specifically apply to financially supporting missionaries and other gospel workers, such as church pastors and elders.

I was surprised to learn that two-thirds of the New Testament references specifying recipients of our giving pertain to helping persecuted and suffering Christians. In hindsight, I should not have been surprised. After all, we know from 1 Corinthians 16:1–2 that the apostle Paul originally initiated Sunday collections in order to collect money for suffering Christians:

Now concerning the collection for the saints, as I have given orders to the churches of Galatia, so you must do also: On the first day of the week let each one of you lay something aside, storing up as he may prosper, that there be no collections when I come. (NKJV)

The first Sunday collections were designated 100 percent for the express purpose of providing aid to suffering Christians living in a foreign land. Contrast that with American Christianity where it is estimated that less than half of 1 percent of our Sunday collections are used to help persecuted Christians. Note that Paul made unmistakably clear in this passage that *caring for suffering Christians isn't optional*—he issued "orders" to this effect to the Galatian and Corinthian believers. And the Lord, through Paul, says to us, "So you must do also."

Yes, I understand that first-century believers also gave offerings for other legitimate purposes, and that today's church budgets can't be (nor should be) 100 percent designated to suffering Christians. My point is to highlight the huge shift in values and priorities. The early church provided aid to persecuted Christians as one of their highest priorities. In sharp contrast, American Christians are culpable of near-complete neglect of our most needy family, even though both the need and the available resources are much greater today.

Neither am I suggesting we should give 66 percent of our offerings to suffering and persecuted Christians, 21 percent to the poor, and 13 percent to missionaries and church leaders (proportional to the number of New Testament verses in each category). However, if preponderance of mention is any indicator of importance to the Lord (and I believe it is), then providing assistance to persecuted and suffering Christians should be our highest or near-highest priority.

THE STATE OF THE CHURCH

After reading these passages and the many other related Scriptures presented in this book, my family and I understood that we needed to help persecuted Christians. So we searched for churches and church-based organizations through whom we could send an offering to help persecuted Christians. We ended up contacting the leaders of the 150 largest Christian churches and the twenty largest Christian denominational organizations. Here is what we learned:

Sadly, only two of the denominations and three of the churches indicated that they include their persecuted brothers and sisters in their ministry purpose and plan. Of these five organizations, only one made this ministry a significant budgetary item. Eight others indicated that they sometimes, albeit infrequently, provide assistance to persecuted Christians.

The truth is that the leading Christian churches and denominations in the wealthiest nation on earth are ignoring the plight of their suffering brothers and sisters. Such negligence is contrary to the biblical mandate to use our wealth and liberty to help the persecuted children of God. It is also contrary to the early church examples in Scripture, where we see that financially assisting the saints in tribulation is the dominant theme of New Testament giving. You will see this borne out as you study the Bible passages referenced throughout this book.

Many believers today do not understand the biblical mandate and priority to help the persecuted saints because the relevant Scriptures are often read and taught without consideration of their context. Consequently, we live in ignorance or forgetfulness of their original meaning and application.

Take, for example, Paul's master treatise on giving—2 Corinthians 8–9. This passage may be the most significant and substantive teaching on giving in the New Testament. Paul wrote it entirely in an effort to raise financial support for Christians in a faraway land who were suffering (probably due to persecution). Paul commended the Corinthian believers for several areas of obedience in their community. Then, to put in perspective their need to provide for the suffering saints, he said:

> Just as you excel in everything—in faith, in speech, in knowledge, in complete earnestness and in your love for us—*see that you also excel in this grace of giving.* (2 Corinthians 8:7)

Paul was comparing the importance of helping suffering Christians with the importance and priority of faith, prophecy and knowledge. In other words, giving to meet the needs of suffering Christians is just as important as all these other areas of faithfulness and obedience. This is only one of numerous related New Testament admonitions to care for persecuted and suffering fellow believers.

Persecution was a major concern for the first-century church. It's far worse today! We're living in a time when more Christians are being martyred, tortured, incarcerated and oppressed for Christ's sake than ever before. Experts disagree sharply on the number of Christians who are killed for their faith every year. Their estimates range from several thousand on the low end to more than one hundred thousand—brothers and sisters murdered every year simply because they love Jesus. The numbers vary primarily because experts disagree in their definitions of what constitutes a Christian and when murder constitutes martyrdom. The exact number isn't important for our purpose in this book. Regardless of how you define martyrdom, countless millions more are, at this very moment, suffering greatly in many other ways for Christ's name's sake.

The church of Jesus is suffering as much as—if not more than—it ever has. That's why the New Testament's teachings on helping persecuted believers are as critically relevant today as when they were first written.

STRUGGLING NOT AGAINST FLESH AND BLOOD

I want to caution you before you read the following story—one of several persecution stories you'll read throughout this book. Perhaps I can best illustrate my point by describing a recent experience.

I was invited to speak at a church on the topic of persecution in the Middle East. After I finished, the senior pastor roused the church to anger against those who persecute Christians. My heart sank in response to his angry tone and words. My message wasn't intended to spotlight evil men, but rather to highlight the circumstances of and encourage compassion for the brothers and sisters in our persecuted family.

Similarly, the stories in this book are presented to encourage you to remember and have compassion for the persecuted body of Christ. If we're not careful, these stories can stir up fear, anger and hate towards those inflicting the harm, as it did to Peter when he cut off Malchus's ear when "defending" Jesus. But the Spirit whispers, "Love your enemies and pray for those who persecute you" (Matthew 5:44). Jesus led the way for us when He was nailed to the cross and prayed, "Father, forgive them, for they do not know what they are doing" (Luke 23:34).

It seems that we have to continually remind ourselves that "our struggle is not against flesh and blood, but against the rulers, against the authorities, against the powers of this dark world and against the spiritual forces of evil in the heavenly realms" (Ephesians 6:12). Our enemy is not Hinduism, Islam, Communism or Buddhism. Nor is it the people who practice these religions.

I will note also that there are more stories in this book about persecution in Islamic nations than under any other belief system. This is not due to any bias on my part. It is because eleven out of the top sixteen countries with the worst records for religious persecution are Islamic nations.[2]

FOR THOUGHT AND DISCUSSION

It's human nature to resist change in ourselves, to resist admitting the need to think differently. Which mental or emotional barriers might you need to confront as you continue this journey? Take a moment to express to the Lord your openness to following His path, wherever He might take you.

Journaling space provided at the end of this book.

REAL LIFE IN LAOS

Exiled for Love and Lord[3]

Katin is a peaceful village. Until Jesus invades.

Family by family, one household at a time, a church grows in the highland village in southern Laos. They build a place of worship. They select a pastor. They openly adore their Lord and Savior.

But as Jesus promised, troubles follow soon. Communist Laos is 1.5 percent Christian and 67 percent Buddhist. The rest of the population are mostly animistic spiritists inhabiting outlying areas like the vicinity of Katin. The villagers fear that the Christians' defections from spirit worship will anger the locality's many powerful spirits, bringing upon the whole village any number of illnesses and other calamities. And so this recent wave of local persecution—which continues to our present day—begins in 2003: Government officials confiscate the church building, forcing our brothers and sisters to start meeting outdoors. Three years later the pastor is murdered. The believers persist in worship.

Two years after that, villagers seize a Christian man named Pew and pour rice wine down his throat. He dies of asphyxiation. The grieving family buries their loved one and places a wooden cross upon his grave—an action village officials condemn as "practicing the rituals of the enemy of the state." They fine the family by taking their water buffalo and a pig. One pig is a devastating loss, but taking a family's buffalo—their beast of burden—is like confiscating a farmer's tractor.

By this time, twenty families in Katin have come to faith in Christ, but over the next few weeks all of them—threatened with eviction and eventual starvation—give in to pressure and sign documents renouncing their faith.

We don't know whether twelve-year-old Sur watched all this from the safety of an unbelieving home or whether his family was one of those who followed Christ. But he was there. He saw. He knew something of the life-changing power of this god and the man named Jesus.

There are no secrets in a village like Katin, and word gets out that some of the believers have begun gathering again for prayer and worship. Neither God's Holy Spirit nor His people will be suppressed.

After Pew's murder, the previously disinterested district and provincial officials come to the Christians' aid . . . *at the orders of the communist Laotian central government.* The officials visit the village in order to clarify the laws of Laos. In persecuting the Christians, they say, the village leaders have violated the country's constitution, which guarantees freedom of religion. Justice and freedom have finally come to Katin.

But once the officials have performed their required duty, they leave the Christians in the hands of the hostile villagers. Four days later the village authorities seize a Christian family's buffalo, offering to return it if the family will renounce their faith. The father refuses, and the next day the officials slaughter the buffalo and distribute the meat to non-Christian families. They promise to continue seizing livestock until there are no more Christians or no more animals belonging to Christians.

Our brothers and sisters worship on. Over the next two years they endure further dire threats and theft of their livestock. Eventually the village chief declares that only spirit worship is acceptable in his village. By now we know that Sur's family has come to faith in Christ.

This sets the scene for the Sunday that marks the turning point of Sur's life.

Fourteen-year-old Sur gasps and stares, watching a hundred hostile villagers and local officials intrude on the Christian worship service about ten o'clock that Sunday morning. Cold fear grips Sur as guns are placed to the heads of various church members. All forty-eight of them—men, women and children from eleven families—are forced out to an open field.

"Renounce your faith!" demand the village leaders, fearing the wrath of angered spirits over the Christians' worship of Jesus. Something inside Sur wonders if they're right. After all, not long ago his now-Christian family routinely sacrificed to the spirits.

Sur turns his frightened gaze to his father and mother, and he sees the solemn resolve on their faces, bolstered by their love and trust for Jesus. He is still afraid, but he strengthens his determination to mimic their conviction. Maybe if he behaves bravely he'll feel braver. It helps a little. He consciously stands taller as the confrontation continues.

No matter what threats and gibes the village leaders scream at the Christians, none will deny Jesus Christ. They hold dear the love and forgiveness of their Lord and the promise of eternity with Him.

Meanwhile, Sur can hear and see the ransacking of the eleven families' homes. Their belongings are thrown carelessly out onto the ground. The villagers confiscate one family's pig, worth six weeks' labor. And then the worst: Six of the Christians' homes are completely destroyed before their eyes.

Sur looks around at his older brother Yead, younger sister Ngoy, and eight-year-old brother Jeed, and at his other friends and their parents. Many are weeping, watching the pillage and destruction of all they own—wanting to intervene, yet mindful of the weapons trained on them. Death rests in the hands of their enemies.

Finally, when the leaders and officials realize they're not succeeding at dissuading any of the Christians from their faith, they once again point their guns directly at the Christians' heads and command them to begin walking along the road out of the village. The bereft and suddenly destitute families snatch up what belongings they can grab and begin the march to a location four miles away, on the edge of the jungle, where they will establish the new "home" they will inhabit for at least the next two years.

Sur is beginning the ordeal that will impact the rest of his life. He and the other forty-seven believers—including two-year-olds and adults as old as sixty—are abandoned virtually empty-handed at the side of the road.

"You may not come back until you renounce Christ," say the officials.

With growing dread Sur realizes, *We have no food. I need water, now. Is there any water here? We can't protect ourselves. No shelter . . . or tools for building or farming. We need our water buffalo to pull the plow. Wait, we have no plow!*

The small community begins immediately searching for food, water and any form of shelter. They anticipate the rains lasting for two more months. Then the bone-chilling mountain temperatures of Laos's dry winter, with no rainwater—only the tiny, polluted trickle of a nearby stream—until late spring or early summer.

That night, Sur sleeps on the hard ground under the most heavily foliaged tree his family can find. These dear friends enter that dark night "speaking to one another in psalms and hymns and spiritual songs, singing and making melody with [their] heart to the Lord; always giving thanks for all things in the name of our Lord Jesus Christ to God, even the Father" (Ephesians 5:19–20, NASB).

They knew it might happen. And still they stuck with Jesus.

Picture these dear Jesus followers building temporary shelters without the benefit of tools, repeatedly ordered to stop building shelters and to sleep on the ground. They refuse. Under the meager protection of a branches-and-grass structure, Sur tries to ignore his hunger and the whimpering of the community's children as he shivers in the cold. Does he sometimes wish his family would just reject Jesus? Who could blame him?

Feel these believers' defeat when, days later, the district official turns against them and declares that he will allow no Christianity on his watch. Or the short-lived thrill when the district official is overruled by the provincial governor, who visits the forty-eight at their jungle refuge and assures them they may worship as they wish and live wherever they please.

But it's only words. Nothing changes.

Imagine the physical condition of our brothers and sisters over the next several months—the multiple diseases they contract from eating whatever animal life and edible vegetation they can find in the jungle, from drinking water unfit for ingestion. For three months they're refused medical treatment, until at last two become so ill that they're allowed hospitalization. Join Sur with his family, huddled in prayer for one of the sick individuals. Feel the bottom drop out of Sur's world as he listens to his father praying, hears his father's labored breathing—then opens his eyes to see his father falter and suddenly die.

The next year and a half is filled with the backs and forths of a spiritual battle turned very physical. Of warfare literally to the death. The families are allowed to retrieve limited quantities of rice from the village, but only enough to stave off complete starvation. Some families return to their hereditary rice fields and begin cultivating, even without buffalos, even though it's off season, just to gain a little extra food and to preserve their right to use the fields under Laotian law. But villagers drain the paddies, burn the protective fences and trample the rice seedlings; officials prohibit the Christians from returning or replanting their former farmland. So the eleven desperate families begin the laborious process of clearing new farming space near their place of exile; persons unknown burn their seed supply and the few farming tools they've acquired or improvised.

Seven more Katin families come to faith in Jesus Christ—two immediately following the original expulsion, four after the villagers threaten to shoot any returning exiles, and one on the heels of new expulsion threats. These fifteen new believers are cast out of the village and are welcomed by the forty-eight, who build additional shelters and cut their own rations to share with their brothers and sisters in need.

Take a moment to reread that last sentence. And marvel.

In February, more than a year after their eviction from the village, comes the beginning of the dry season.

The exiled Katin Christians, numbering sixty-two, are so utterly defeated they resort to begging for food. Authorities defy their own nation's constitution, circulating word to all nearby villages that no one should help the "lawbreaking" Christians.

By July, the outcasts are still dependent on outside support. But the rains have come, their new fields are growing rice, and their health has greatly improved. Some of the children are allowed to attend school in a nearby township, and more believers are coming out of the Katin village woodwork, quietly visiting the refugees for worship.

September: Five new Katin families have come to faith in Christ, and three of the exiled families return to the village to join them. Village officials can't ignore this; they demand a fine of one pig per family.

At this point we lose word of Sur and the rest of the church at Katin. No further mention of their situation is found in available Internet articles as of the time of this writing.

Katin is only one of hundreds or thousands of variations on the same theme, travesties being perpetrated *today* against the hundred thousand Christians in Laos—one of the world's worst countries for human rights violations and persecution of Christians.[4]

CHAPTER 3

Missing in Inaction

If Christians are being persecuted and murdered on such a cruel and massive scale, you might be wondering, *why don't we know it?*

Except for recent reporting about ISIS (Islamic State in Iraq and Syria), mainstream media and most politicians have ignored virtually all the horrific news about Christian persecution. When secular media sources do report on situations involving Christian persecution, they often hide the truth by inaccurately and vaguely describing such events as "terrorism" or "tribal," "sectarian" or "political" conflicts, rather than attacks on Christians. Even many US church leaders avoid talking about persecution for fear of jeopardizing their multicultural evangelistic initiatives, or because it is "a downer," according to a Barna Research Associates survey of American pastors.[5] Although Christian persecution is the most pervasive and severe violation of human rights in the world, so few people—even Christians in the US, with our access to information—know much about it.

Because mainstream news sources report tragedies like the ongoing massacre in Nigeria as merely "terrorism" or "sectarian violence," most American Christians do not know that twenty thousand people, mostly Christians, have been brutally murdered in northern Nigeria since Sharia law was instituted in 2010. Or that 2.5 million—mostly Christians—are now homeless because of violence or threats of violence against them.

We can't rely on mainstream secular media or many of our politicians to provide us with accurate and complete persecution-related news. Persecution news is available to a limited degree on the Internet. However, most Christian persecution is never reported anywhere, because local authorities often sympathize with the persecutors and refuse to assist Christians or allow their stories to be made known. Local officials often subject Christians to further oppression just for crying out to the world and seeking help.

Still, the reliable news sources we *do* have provide us with ample evidence that a staggering number of our spiritual family members around the globe are being severely mistreated for loving Jesus. Equipped with this awareness, what then is our obligation before God?

It's the same as it was two thousand years ago, at a time when "heirloom love" was simply known as . . . love.

SAME SITUATION, DIFFERENT DAY

They stoned Stephen. . . . And on that day a great persecution began against the church in Jerusalem, and they were all scattered throughout the regions of Judea and Samaria, except the apostles. (Acts 7:59; 8:1, NASB)

After Stephen was murdered, people throughout Jerusalem took up arms against the followers of Jesus.

According to Acts, there were apparently more than ten thousand believers in Jesus by the time of Stephen's martyrdom.[6] Imagine the multiple hardships implied when we read that "they were all scattered" throughout the surrounding regions. Fleeing for their lives, thousands of families left behind their homes, their livelihoods, their extended families and support networks. Today in the West, we can fall back on temporary housing and on help to find new employment. But these people literally faced a life-and-death quandary as they attempted to resettle in strange lands. Who would come to their aid? The uncaring Roman government? No. The majority of fellow Jews, who disbelieved the claims of Jesus? No. They were dependent solely on the mercy of other Jesus followers to provide them with food and shelter.

It's in this context that we're meant to read most or all of the New Testament admonitions to hospitality—specifically for the sake of Jesus' homeless followers who were being persecuted for loving Him.

> Do not neglect to show hospitality to strangers, for by this some have entertained angels without knowing it. (Hebrews 13:2, NASB)

> Offer hospitality to one another without grumbling. (1 Peter 4:9)

Commands such as these were written specifically to exhort the more fortunate believers to provide life-sustaining aid to Christian refugees who had been driven from their homes by persecution. Let's be careful not to redefine or minimize these teachings to mean merely having friends over for lunch after church.

FROM THE ENDS OF THE EARTH

So if a persecuted Christian knocks at my door, God commands me to help him or her. But you're talking about persecuted Christians on the other side of the world.

Yes, you're right. The first line of aid for the Jerusalem refugees was the believers in the regions to which they fled—Judea and Samaria. But the Church, the one unified body of Christ, is much larger, and Jesus intends that His worldwide Church come to the aid of His suffering people.

> The disciples were called Christians first at Antioch. . . . The disciples, each according to his ability, decided to provide help for the brothers living in Judea. This they did, sending their gift to the elders by Barnabas and Saul. (Acts 11:26,29–30)

The regions of Judea and Samaria were within two or three days' travel of Jerusalem. Antioch, on the other hand, was three hundred miles to the north—a good two-week journey. This was nowhere in the neighborhood. In fact, conveyance of a financial gift today from the United States to any other point in the world is much easier than it was for Barnabas and Saul to carry this gift three hundred miles from Antioch to Jerusalem. And the Christians of Antioch were even less likely ever to meet one of the brothers or sisters they helped than you are to meet a persecuted brother or sister from Asia or Africa. And still they helped. Distance didn't matter. Cultural and linguistic differences didn't count. Only their oneness in Jesus was meaningful, and they did what family does.

Paul is known for numerous "collections for the saints." This was probably the first. Later he would collect money for suffering saints from Christians who lived even farther away—in modern-day Turkey and Greece.[7]

As we will see later, Peter, James and John all gave similar instructions to Christians—to provide for the physical needs of suffering fellow believers.

What about you? What about your church? It's my hope that as a result of considering what I'm sharing, you might reexamine your giving and priorities in the light of the Scriptures presented in this book.

Even a small (and growing) number of committed believers can radically multiply the help that's currently going to our oppressed family.

FOR THOUGHT AND DISCUSSION

Previously, when you've read the New Testament's instructions about hospitality, to whom have you thought to apply them? Now that you know they were first intended to benefit persecuted Christian refugees, how does that affect your thinking and plans about how you will obey them?

Journaling space provided at the end of this book.

Worship from a Metal Box

Picture a scene of rocky desert on the southern outskirts of Africa's Sahara. No vegetation, not even a scrub bush in sight. Clouds are rare, the sun beats down on every square inch and daytime temperatures commonly top 90 degrees F, sometimes climbing to a searing 100 and higher.

Now put a metal shipping container in the middle of this flat, desolate landscape—a truck-sized steel box like one that might be loaded onto a train or a ship. Its battered, oxidized surface absorbs the sun's rays and creates an ovenlike environment inside. This container sits sealed shut, out in the desert heat day after day after day.

Next imagine eighteen or twenty emaciated men or women crammed into this metal container, confined continuously for weeks and months and years, their bodies baking all day long, gasping for breaths of fresh air through one paperback-book-sized hole in the wall.

Finally, picture dozens of such shipping containers arrayed across the parched landscape, "housing" hundreds of suffering people. This is Mai Serwa prison camp outside Asmara, Eritrea.

This is also a site of sacred worship. The rusty containers comprise a cathedral of sorts, housing among the inmates an unknown number of Jesus followers and seekers, a flock of spiritual sheep. Their number is strong and growing, in large part because just a few years ago their shepherd was a frail thirty-year-old woman named Helen Berhane.

Helen always loved her country—a small, war-torn nation on the east coast of Africa. Its population is nearly half Muslim and nearly half Orthodox Christian. The government allows practice of these and the Catholic and Lutheran faiths, but evangelical Christianity was outlawed in 2002. The paranoid government suspects evangelical Christians to be spies against the state; thus these brothers and sisters are granted no freedom to congregate, worship or even possess a Bible.

Eritrea is known as the "North Korea of Africa" for its brutal treatment of its own citizens. Twenty thousand people are currently imprisoned there without charge or trial. These include, at any one time, an estimated 10 percent of Eritrea's evangelical Christians; 50 percent of the nation's Christians have been imprisoned at some time during their lives. Why? Because their consciences prompt them to worship according to a tradition differing from those allowed by the government.

It was in this hostile context that the Lord called Helen to serve as a shepherd caring for His sheep. Ever since her childhood she knew she was meant to serve the Lord with her life, and in her late twenties she found herself leading and teaching a flock of hungry followers.

And she sang. Oh, how she sang! The Holy Spirit gifted Helen to inspire others through her songwriting and singing. In fact, she published an album of worship songs that proved popular among Eritreans; it was distributed widely through the underground churches.

Then one night, as our sister was teaching in a secret church meeting, she was arrested in a raid. Helen's punishment for the crime of worshipping in an unauthorized church was thirty-one straight months of imprisonment, most of it in her shipping container home in the desert. When Helen arrived at Mai Serwa prison camp, she discovered that inmates were kept sealed in their containers most of the time. Once or twice per day she was allowed to use the "toilet"—a flat, open area of rocky ground a half-mile from camp. Otherwise she had to use a bucket in one corner of her container. Men and women were segregated into separate containers, though one of the most frightening punishments for a female inmate was to be forced to sleep among the male prisoners; rape and a resulting pregnancy would almost certainly kill the woman in the camp's harsh conditions. Inmates were shuffled around and sometimes crammed together with more bodies than space permits to sleep at one time on the uneven floor. So they would sleep in shifts, rotating to preferred locations, away from the stagnant puddles from dripping condensation and farthest from the stench from the toilet bucket.

Helen's diet varied unpredictably and was never adequate for sustaining health. Sometimes the food was purposefully made inedible, by over-salting, for example. Medics were available merely to keep prisoners alive, not to keep them healthy.

Guards regularly punished inmates for making noise, for looking out of the breathing hole, or just because a guard was having a bad day. Christian prisoners received the worst treatment in the camp. Every time new prisoners arrived, a Christian—often Helen herself—was brought out and tortured as an example intended to frighten the new prisoners into submission.

Throughout her imprisonment, officials used beatings, exposure to the extreme heat and cold, and other forms of torture to pressure her to recant her faith. Repeatedly she was offered freedom; she need only sign a document promising forever to discontinue her ministry activities. Repeatedly she refused. Instead, Helen persisted in singing praises, teaching the Bible, praying with others and smuggling Scripture-based messages of truth and encouragement. She was caught and punished many times, and at each turn this simple-hearted, steadfast sister courageously declared her intention to continue obeying her Lord.

Helen had once read Richard Wurmbrand's *Tortured for Christ*, in which the author wrote of his experience in prison: "We could not be prevented from singing, although we were beaten for this. I imagine that nightingales, too, would sing, even if they knew that after finishing they would be killed for it." Helen found it impossible *not* to sing.

Helen sang of the brave heroes of the Bible, who looked forward to a better country.[8]

At the same time she loved her earthly country, Eritrea, whose government punished her for her loyalty.

Helen sang about peace and joy from the Lord—both so valuable that no earthly loss could compare.

Her torturers could only shake their heads in bewilderment.

Helen sang about hope and salvation, even for her tormentors.

Her jailers shouted all the louder to drown out her message—but some were listening, learning.

Helen sang about love and forgiveness. She loved and prayed for her guards and even felt sorry for them; in some ways this was as much a prison for them as it was for her. Spies were recruited to trap Helen with evidence of her persistent "wrongdoing." Instead, she won them over with love and the Lord's truth; they would not betray her.

A few of the guards secretly joined Helen's flock, learning about Jesus and God's Word. Helen continued to write Bible lessons for prisoners throughout the camp—Christians and not-yet-Christians alike—smuggling them around and receiving smuggled messages in return. Her ministry helped rescue many from eternal darkness, from suicide, from depression, from the traps of hatred and bitterness.

The reputations of Helen and other Christians became well known throughout Mai Serwa, and former skeptics began to wonder about this Jesus for whom someone would endure so much.

Finally, after catching Helen smuggling a Bible message, officials became so exasperated that one of the camp chiefs—a Muslim named Suleiman, well known for his methodical torture—called Helen before him. She wasn't chained; everyone at Mai Serwa knew Christians didn't fight back.

Suleiman trembled with rage. A police baton lay at hand. Helen trembled with terror in spite of her faith. Suleiman raised the baton to strike.

Helen raised her eyes to Jesus, the Lamb who remained silent even when beaten.[9]

Suleiman systematically beat Helen over every inch of her body.

By her Lord's grace, Helen endured in silence. Not a cry, not a whimper.

"Leave us alone, Helen!" Suleiman began to scream, in rhythm with his fearsome blows.

Helen's existence was nothing but agony and Jesus.

Suleiman became so fatigued he had to rest. Then he resumed.

When he'd finished, Suleiman had Helen dragged back and chained in the searing sun outside her container. She knew she was dying; she would soon see Jesus.

Camp medics discovered Helen's condition; one of them, seeing her head-to-toe wounds, had to leave the examination room to cry.

Over the next several days the medics, fearful of a death on their watch, implored Suleiman to send Helen to the Asmara hospital. Suleiman refused; he was trying to cover up his actions.

Helen deteriorated, losing blood, unable to stand, eventually unable to urinate. Her breathing was restricted by swelling in her neck. She lay for days in her container, praying for Suleiman's repentance and salvation and continuing, as she was able, to write Bible lessons and messages of encouragement for her flock. The mistreatment continued—even another beating. Throughout her endless torment, the Lord's nightingale sang.

Then came the day Suleiman relented, and Helen was released. She had been in prison for thirty-one months and two weeks.

With proper medical treatment and the attentive care of her family, Helen slowly recovered in the hospital. But she was not out of danger. In light of the near-certainty that she would be re-incarcerated as soon as she was well, Helen escaped from her beloved country, miraculously, to neighboring Sudan, where her sister cared for her.

Helen soon learned that she was not yet beyond the clutches of the Eritrean authorities. She moved to secret locations several times, but each time she began to receive anonymous threatening phone calls.

She applied to several nations for asylum and finally found security and freedom in a new home, Denmark.

Helen has shared her story in a book titled *Song of the Nightingale.* She still loves her home country and longs for a day when the powers of darkness there no longer crush the sons of light. Perhaps that day will come by way of the collective voices of Western Christians and other freedom lovers.

To this day Helen continues her ministry wherever and however the Lord leads her.

She has never stopped singing.[10]

CHAPTER 4

A New Creature

I lived an irresponsible and destructive lifestyle until I was twenty-eight years old. I was drowning in debt, past-due on seemingly countless credit card accounts. Something needed to change in my life, but trying harder to change, I found myself sliding deeper into sin. Lost in the misery of fleshly living, I finally realized my desperate need for grace, to be saved from my sins. With the help of a friend named Dale, I understood that Christ died to pay the penalty for my wrongs and to set me free from sin so I might live a new life in Him.

Once I became a Christian, God's grace redeemed my past mistakes and gave me clarity for walking in His wisdom. In my zeal for handling money God's way, I decided to give a small amount from each paycheck to my local church. Though it was a mere token, it was significant to me. At the time, the minimum payments on my credit cards totaled more than my income, and creditors were calling me almost daily. Giving an offering of any amount was a sacrifice.

The day after I gave my first offering, I found a large stack of hundred- and fifty-dollar bills that someone had misplaced. I immediately called both my pastor and my best friend, Paul, an attorney, and asked what I should do with the money. They both told me to call the police. Go ahead, nominate me for the "Duh" Award for even needing to ask. But I did need to ask. This was new territory for me. Before Jesus saved me, I would have claimed "finders keepers" and kept the money.

After I called the police, a detective was dispatched to pick up the money and prepare a report. The detective told me they would have to conduct an investigation, and the money would be returned to me if they didn't find the owner within ninety days.

I spent the next ninety days planning how to spend "my" money. I went shopping and picked out a new speedboat and a wardrobe of new clothes. It never occurred to me, despite their frequent phone reminders, that I might use the money to pay my creditors. At the end of the ninety days, I inquired about the money. The detective told me they hadn't started the investigation and it was going to take another ninety days.

On the Sunday after I received this news, my church started a six-week stewardship program. After the second Sunday of this program, I finally understood that all the money in my possession belongs to the Lord, and I'm responsible for using His money to accomplish His purposes. I'm a steward, a manager—not an owner. I vowed that if the police gave the money back to me, I wouldn't spend it without first seeking the Lord's purpose for it.

The next day—yes, the next day—the detective called and said they'd completed the investigation early. The money was mine! After seeking to know the Lord's will for it, I gave an offering to my church and used the remainder to repay my debts.

Imagine that! No speedboat or new clothes in the Lord's plan for me!

Through this experience I came to the scriptural conclusion that we have a responsibility to live modestly in order to give as much as possible for building up the body of Christ and helping the poor. I vowed to the Lord that should He ever increase my income, I would not increase my consumption or standard of living. Instead, I would donate more toward building up His body and helping the poor.

It was easy for me to make that commitment, because at that time in my life my wife, Debbie, and I were content with spending less than we were earning. We were living in a modest home, driving modest cars, taking simple vacations, occasionally dining out at inexpensive restaurants, and we were able to purchase the things we needed. Little did I know that just six months later the Lord was going to put my word to the test—by blessing me. That's when my friends and I started a technology company that became very successful and went public on NASDAQ during the tech boom of the 1990s.

THE GRADUATE SCHOOL OF OBEDIENCE

Money is like an acid test that penetrates our exterior religious veneer and reveals the true condition of our hearts. From firsthand experience, I know this to be true because I failed the test. I sold my stock in our company, and I broke my pledge not to increase my consumption and standard of living. I conveniently adopted the popular teaching that says "ten percent for God and ninety percent for me." I gave ten percent of the stock sale proceeds to my local church—plus an additional ten percent of "my" money to various charities—in an ill-fated attempt to placate my conscience for indulging myself with the remaining eighty percent.

I fooled myself into believing that I should build a new waterfront home that was five times larger than our previous comfortable home. I tried to convince Debbie that we needed this house "in order to do the Lord's work," such as hosting Bible studies and outreach activities. Debbie didn't share my vision, so it was against her counsel that I built the house. This was one of the biggest mistakes I've ever made.

Shortly after we moved into our new home, I was bitten by a tick while on a church camping trip. A few days later, I developed a Lyme disease rash, and within two weeks I began to experience other severe symptoms of the disease. I was infected with a particularly aggressive strain that did not respond to antibiotics. My health declined rapidly. Within eighteen months I looked like a walking skeleton. I developed severe arthritis so debilitating that I had great difficulty getting out of bed. My fatigue became so great that walking any distance—even from one side of our home to the other—was a chore. Our spacious new house felt like a curse.

The Lyme disease caused me to forget what I was saying, and I could not finish my sentences. I lost the tissue that padded my seat and the bottoms of my feet, so sitting or standing was painful without pillows and special padding in my shoes. My spine and joints cracked loudly when I moved.

I developed liver complications and candida from excessive antibiotics. The candida caused intestinal and digestion issues, as well as a thick white thrush coating that grew on my tongue and blackish green fungus that grew in my nails. As if I didn't look pitiful enough already, red bumps the size of pencil erasers grew on my head and neck.

Yes, this was the life.

Shortly after I became sick, the Lord revealed to me that the disease was no accident; He was disciplining me for my unfaithfulness with His money (Hebrews 12:5–11). I had tried to hijack His story and make it about me. So He dragged me kicking and screaming into my own private wilderness that He might have all my attention. He got it. I repented of my unfaithfulness, and the Lord set me free from bondage to money—a counterfeit master who promised to satisfy my soul, but who would betray me every time. The Lord healed me of a spiritual ailment that had harmed me more severely than my physical ailment—it had turned my heart away from Him.

Once again the joy of the Lord became my strength. Outwardly I continued to waste away, but inwardly I was being renewed day by day.

Just to be clear, I don't believe that every negative circumstance is a sign of the Lord's discipline for sin, nor that every positive circumstance is evidence of His blessing for obedience. Learning to discern the Lord's intention in our circumstances is a matter of prayer, careful consideration and wise counsel.

THE GRACE OF A SECOND CHANCE

My ordeal had now lasted eighteen months. My health continued to deteriorate, and Debbie and I were losing hope. We believed my earthly days were coming to end. I wasted away to the point that my bones were sticking out. Debbie and my mother could hardly look at me without crying.

About this time a sister in the Lord gave me a sermon video and another friend gave me a book—both about boldly and persistently crying out to Lord, with childlike wailing, until He comes to our rescue (see Luke 18:1–8). I was desperate. During the next three weeks I went to a quiet place where no one else could hear me, and every day I mourned, lamented and wailed loudly, pleading with the Lord to heal me. I literally carried on like a desperate child who was lost in the wilderness, scared and about to die.

After three weeks of crying out, I received a call from a faithful brother in the Lord named Alex. He said the Lord had just told him to call and tell me He was going to heal me. At that moment, the Lord did exactly that! He healed me. Hallelujah! All the Lyme disease symptoms immediately left my body. My memory, liver and digestive issues returned to normal. The red bumps, thrush and fungus disappeared, and I had energy for the first time in eighteen months. I felt like I'd been raised from a living death.

Through my recovery the Lord was telling me, Your part in My story isn't finished yet, son. I have more for you to do for Me here on earth. I renewed my resolve to love and serve the Lord with all my heart, soul, mind and strength—and with whatever wealth He entrusted to me. This was the beginning of my journey to finding heirloom love.

BY GRACE THROUGH FAITH

While we're on the topic of the Lord's astounding grace in my life, I want to clarify a potential error in thinking. If you were to read only the Scriptures quoted in this book concerning our responsibility to minister to suffering and persecuted Christians, you could get the impression that salvation can be earned by helping the least of the saints.

However, we know by reading the whole Bible that this is far from the truth. We must first be changed by God's grace, through faith, and then we can live in obedience to Him. The person who reads these verses and thinks that they can be saved from their sins by living righteously has confused cause and effect.

Take for example the following passage:

> Then the King will say to those on his right, "Come, you who are blessed by my Father; take your inheritance, the kingdom prepared for you since the creation of the world. For I was hungry and you gave me something to eat, I was thirsty and you gave me something to drink. . . ."
>
> Then the righteous will answer him, "Lord, when did we see you hungry and feed you, or thirsty and give you something to drink? . . ."
>
> The King will reply, "I tell you the truth, whatever you did for one of the least of these brothers of mine, you did for me." (Matthew 25:34–40)

Some might read this teaching of Jesus and think that the "righteous" became righteous (and earned salvation) by serving needy Christians—that good works make a person righteous.

However the Bible tells us clearly that one must be saved from his sins and be made righteous by an act of God alone—not by anything we can do.

> A man is not justified by observing the law, but by faith in Jesus Christ. (Galatians 2:16)

Justification before God happens when one is born again, and this rebirth occurs by God's grace, through our faith. It's not earned by our good works.

> It is by grace you have been saved, through faith—and this not from yourselves, it is the gift of God—not by works, so that no one can boast. (Ephesians 2:8-9)

It's God's gift of righteousness that transforms a person into someone who, by nature, does good works like serving the needy. Look at the very next verse in Ephesians 2:

For we are God's workmanship, created in Christ Jesus to do good works, which God prepared in advance for us to do. (2:10)

We aren't saved by good works; we're saved in order to do good works. A lifestyle of good works follows naturally in the life of a person who has been forgiven and made righteous by God. Through faith in Jesus Christ we're born again and become new creatures that will increasingly conform to the likeness of Jesus Christ (2 Corinthians 5:17, NASB; Romans 8:29). The good deeds we do as we grow in the likeness of Jesus Christ are the effects of salvation and the proof that we've been saved. They're not the cause of our rebirth. Jesus said,

By this my Father is glorified, that you bear much fruit and so prove to be my disciples. (John 15:8, ESV)

The righteous in Matthew 25 proved that they truly were Jesus' disciples by their love and ministry to the needy saints. The same is true today. We prove we're already Jesus' disciples by, among other things, our love and deeds on behalf of the suffering and persecuted saints.

FOR THOUGHT AND DISCUSSION

When eternity is on the line, it can't hurt to stop and ask yourself, "Have I really got it right? Do I understand how to be saved?"

If you have any doubt, prayerfully reread the Scriptures quoted in this chapter. Are you depending solely on the payment of Jesus' life for your forgiveness—as the Bible teaches—or are you depending on yourself or anything else?

Journaling space provided at the end of this book.

PART II

—⁂—

LOVE FOUND

—⁂—

A new command I give you:
Love one another. As I have loved you,
so you must love one another.

—Jesus, John 13:34

CHAPTER 5

Love One Another

What do you do when the Author of the Ten Commandments says, "I have a new commandment for you"?

Think about it. Imagine yourself one of Jesus' closest earthly friends, sitting by His side on that fateful night when He was about to be arrested and crucified. The Messiah spends the evening with you, sharing His final and most important teachings (John 13–17). And on this evening, among His many teachings and reassurances, Jesus says, "I'm about to give you a new commandment."

What? No one has added to Israel's commandments since the time of Moses! After the first five books—the "Books of Moses"—the rest of the Old Testament serves to clarify, illustrate and interpret the commandments given through Moses. But no new commandments have been added throughout the whole of God's revealed Word.

Until this night.

Tonight the Word Incarnate sits beside you. Just as He did thousands of years ago, when He revealed His heart through His commandments to Israel, so again tonight He speaks. His new command: "Love one another. As I have loved you, so you must love one another" (John 13:34).

This command is the heartbeat we've seemingly lost, the DNA of heirloom love. When it comes to the core teachings that guide the Christian lifestyle, Jesus' new command belongs at the very center. At least, that's what the apostle John seemed to think, as we'll see. And who would know the true heart of the Messiah better than one of His closest friends, one of His inner circle of three, the one to whom Jesus entrusted the care of His mother after His death? It's through John's gospel and his letters that we receive Jesus' new command.

It's significant that Jesus focused His final instructions to His disciples on this one command and that He repeated it *four times* that night—twice in John 13:34, then twice more:

> My command is this: Love each other as I have loved you. Greater love has no one than this, that he lay down his life for his friends. . . . This is my command: Love each other. (John 15:12–13,17)

These were Jesus' final directives to the disciples, as if He were saying to them (and to us), "I'm now leaving you, and if you don't do anything else between now and when I return, make sure that you love one another!"

UNPACKING THE COMMAND

Jesus' new command includes several important implications. First, it's a *command*; His followers, including you and me, are required to obey it. Next, Jesus was commanding us to love "one another"—that is, to love fellow believers. John confirmed this several times in his letter (1 John 1:7–11; 3:10–23; 4:20–21). Jesus did not mean to prohibit love for unbelievers. In fact, He taught exactly the opposite (for example, in Matthew 5:43–47). But He emphasized caring for our brothers and sisters in the faith as our highest priority. Paul confirmed and reinforced this priority when he wrote, "Let us do good to all people, especially to those who belong to the family of believers" (Galatians 6:10).

Jesus commanded us to love each other "as I have loved you." How did Jesus love us?

First, He loved us *unconditionally*. That's at the root of the Greek word *agapē*, which John uses in all these passages to quote Jesus. Jesus didn't wait for us to do something worthy of His love (we couldn't). Instead He took the initiative and loved us first. His love wasn't "I will love you *if*" or "I'll love you *when*"; it was simply, "*I love you.*" That's the kind of love Jesus commands us to exercise toward fellow believers—particularly those who are suffering around the world.

Second, Jesus also loved us *sacrificially*. He went so far as to instruct us specifically to "lay down our lives" for each other (John 15:12–13). He then demonstrated this love only a few hours later by laying down His life for us. John reinforced this point in his epistle to make it unmistakably clear that our priority should be to give our all for the saints in need and, if necessary, even risk our physical lives for their sakes: "This is how we know what love is: Jesus Christ laid down his life for us. And we ought to lay down our lives for our brothers" (1 John 3:16).

Loving fellow believers may cost us something deep and personal. But the more we attain the Lord's perspective and heart, the less it feels like sacrifice. Jesus said that we would be full of joy—His joy—as we obey His new command (John 15:11). The early church was full of His joy because they were committed to helping the persecuted saints.

The Macedonian churches were enduring a "most severe trial" and "extreme poverty." But their joy was "overflowing" because of their love and "rich generosity" for suffering Christians in a foreign land. Their love and joy was so great that "they urgently pleaded with us for the privilege of sharing in this service to the saints" (2 Corinthians 8:1–4). As heirloom love takes root and grows in our hearts, we too will joyfully plead with the Lord for opportunities to give ourselves away.

FOR THOUGHT AND DISCUSSION

Write your own paraphrase of Jesus' command: "Love one another. As I have loved you, so you must love one another." Clarify what He meant by each component of the command.

Journaling space provided at the end of this book.

REAL LIFE IN PAKISTAN

Rape of Innocence

Anna isn't her real name, but in every important way on that Friday morning she was just like any other twelve-year-old girl of any name. She played. She dreamed. She laughed and cried. She was young enough still to harbor elements of a child's innocent outlook upon the world.

She was young enough to trust.

It was Christmas Eve, and Anna's home, like most Christian homes in Lahore, Pakistan, was probably decorated inside with locally crafted trinkets and a tree, and outside with a "star of Bethlehem" on the roof. Perhaps during the preceding week she had participated in caroling from home to home, or maybe she'd given coins rewarding carolers who had come to her home. She was certainly anticipating the celebration that would begin that midnight, as well as the church services and family gatherings of Christmas Day itself.

That Christmas Eve morning a Muslim neighbor girl—one of Anna's friends—came by and invited Anna to go shopping.

Together they headed out. Maybe Anna contemplated buying gifts for her family: special Christmas treats or a decoration for the house. Her friend led her to a car occupied by two strange Muslim men, one of whom the friend introduced as her uncle. The girls got into the car.

We can only imagine at what point Anna realized her shopping trip was turning into something else. Maybe it was when the car left familiar territory and continued on. Maybe it was when she was warned to keep silent. Maybe it was when she was led—perhaps naively, or perhaps against her will—into a strange house.

Over the next two days multiple men raped her. And her ordeal had only begun.

Keep in mind: Anna was *twelve years old.*

On the day after Christmas, three women and Anna's "friend" came to her, promising her release if she would sign some papers. Only the promise of freedom convinced her to sign. She didn't realize that she had just "consented" to marry one of her rapists, a man named Muhammad Irfan.

Anna was never released. For more than eight months she was kept imprisoned, moved from place to place, and repeatedly raped. She was forced to convert to Islam in order to become a suitable wife. When she insisted on remaining faithful to Jesus Christ, she was beaten. By Islamic teaching, her refusal was no barrier to her being made a Muslim, and she was forced to marry Muhammad Irfan.

Anna's family, frantic to find their daughter, had no idea who had kidnapped her. So they filed a complaint "against unknown people" with local police in Lahore. The police took no action. After all, these were only Christians.

Finally, in early September, Anna escaped her captors. She hid out at a bus stop and called her parents from a public telephone. The family traveled more than a hundred miles to Faisalabad to retrieve her. Back in Lahore they brought Anna before a local magistrate, who recorded Anna's statement, but refused to assign protection or even to order a medical exam for Anna.

The rapists—shamelessly unafraid of being identified—appealed to police, presenting a marriage certificate as "proof " that Anna was now a Muslim and married to one of the group. Now equipped with the names of the criminals, Anna's family returned to the police to amend their formal complaint to include the perpetrators' names. The response: No. We won't let you do that. In fact, you need to be reasonable. Everyone concerned will be better off when you return the girl to her "legal" husband. If you don't, you'll be considered criminals; a case will be filed against you.

All this despite the fact that Pakistani law forbids marriage under age sixteen—as well as kidnapping, rape, beatings and false accusation.

Since then, according to the latest available records, neither Anna nor her family have been able to return to their home; they're on the run from her captors, from the police, and possibly from a terrorist group with whom her rapists are allegedly associated. If the family is found, they could lose their freedom or their lives.

What if you were Anna's mother or father, or her brother or sister? Consider for a moment what these circumstances mean for these very real people, treated in these ways simply because they choose to love Jesus. They've left behind their home, their possessions, their friends, their way of life. What would these losses mean to you?

And what about Anna? Hopeless and violated for what seemed like eternity, is she afraid to close her eyes because of the horrors that fill her dreams at night? The emotional barriers that now hinder her from ever accepting herself or trusting a man must seem insurmountable. Will she ever believe she's worth anything, or will she see herself as forever ruined, destined merely to endure the deep lonely ache throughout her remaining days, years, decades?

The word *tragedy* seems too tame to describe Anna's ordeal and its aftermath. But her story is happening all over Pakistan to other Annas. In this country where women have especially low social status, some estimate that seven hundred Christian girls and women each year are kidnapped, raped, forcibly converted to Islam and forcibly married to their captors. Since 99 percent of rape cases in Pakistan are never reported,[11] the actual number of victims is probably many times that conservative estimate. Every year. Year after year.

One Muslim cleric, while solemnizing a forced marriage, declared the rapist's behavior to be "a pious act" because he had "saved" his victim, bringing her into Islam. When the Christian father of a sixteen-year-old rape victim complained to police, he was kidnapped, shackled, tortured and left in critical condition. In one village in Punjab Province, when Christians objected "too strenuously" to the daily sexual assaults on their women and girls, Muslim leaders ordered 250 Christian families to leave the village and their homes. (The village was first founded by Christians around 1950.)

This disturbing and increasing practice of sexual predation is only one of many tools used by the Muslim majority in Pakistan to persecute Christ's followers there. Homes and property may be seized. Christians are often discriminated against and harassed at their places of work. And Christian students are often publicly ridiculed and even beaten, simply because they love Jesus.

Among the weapons wielded against Christians in Pakistan are its often misused blasphemy laws. Many Muslims, wishing to settle personal vendettas against Christians, have manufactured blasphemy lawsuits against them. These laws include statutes that prohibit "injuring religious feelings," "defiling the Quran" and "blaspheming Muhammad." The first two carry a maximum penalty of life imprisonment, and the last a possible death sentence.

Imagine yourself a follower of Jesus in Pakistan. You read in God's Word that faithfulness to Him means not just worshipping Him and following His example, but also telling others about Jesus and His love. But obeying the Lord's Commission is to risk the possibility of being charged with blasphemy against Islam. Imagine this uncertain daily existence for those who seek to live in faithfulness and obedience to the Lord.

Hundreds of thousands of Christians in Pakistan are so impoverished they're virtual slaves, indebted to Muslim landlords. When they encounter persecution or are accused of breaking some law, few can afford to miss a day of work to go to court, let alone afford the cost of an attorney. One way desperate Christians raise money is by selling one of their kidneys; they're exploited by a burgeoning illegal transplant industry in the country. Thousands of Christians are believed to have sold kidneys to pay off debts. But often the money promised to the donor is unpaid or paid only in part; often unskilled surgeons perform the operations and patients cannot afford proper follow-up care. Many Christians who take this dangerous risk fall seriously ill and die. Let us give thanks for our liberty and remember our brothers and sisters in Pakistan, enduring impossible circumstances simply to survive in one of the world's most hostile and oppressive countries toward Christians.

And especially at Christmas, remember Anna, whose dream Christmas became a nightmare. Pray that she and thousands of girls and women like her might find protection, healing and peace in their heavenly Protector's arms.

Pray that Anna might laugh again.[12]

CHAPTER 6

Loving Them
Is Loving Him

It should be enough that Jesus commanded us to love each other. But we have a tendency to subconsciously filter the Lord's commands, paying attention to certain ones while neglecting others. Sadly, I did this for years with Jesus' new command. But through my difficult experiences I'm learning how critical it is that we *agapē* love each other.

In order that we might fully appreciate the importance of His new command, Jesus explained that our *agapē* love for the saints is inextricably related to our love for Him: "If you love me, you will obey what I command. . . . This is my command: Love each other" (John 14:15; 15:17). The implication in context is that our utmost expression of love for Jesus is our fulfillment of His new command, loving each other.

Concrete, practical, in-the-flesh love for fellow believers is the same as love for Jesus Himself. This is what Jesus was saying in Matthew 25:34–40, when He said that those who care for "the least of these brothers of mine" are ministering directly to Jesus the King. When we minister in any way to persecuted and suffering saints, we are really ministering to the Lord Jesus Christ.

Conversely, when opponents persecute Christians, they are really persecuting Jesus. When the apostle Paul (then named Saul) was stopped by a dazzling light and a booming voice on the road to Damascus, he was in the middle of a systematic campaign to hunt down, imprison and if necessary execute the followers of Jesus. But when he asked the obviously supernatural being, "Who are you, Lord?" the voice answered, "I am Jesus, whom you are persecuting" (Acts 9:5).

Jesus says to us, His followers, "He who rejects you rejects me" (Luke 10:16). And many years after his conversion, Paul would write, "When you sin against your brothers . . . you sin against Christ" (1 Corinthians 8:12).

But sin against Jesus need not be only through persecution of His followers—a sin of *commission,* actively doing what is wrong. We also sin against Jesus by our sin of *omission* when we passively fail to do what is right. When we stand before our Lord and Judge, it won't be enough to stammer, "But I didn't hurt anyone." He will require an accounting of whether we acted upon the many opportunities He has given us to do good. Jesus made it clear that forgetting or passively neglecting the needs of "the least of these" is equivalent to rejecting Him.

> Then he will say to those on his left, "Depart from me, you who are cursed, into the eternal fire prepared for the devil and his angels. For I was hungry and you gave me nothing to eat, I was thirsty and you gave me nothing to drink, I was a stranger [refugee] and you did not invite me in, I needed clothes and you did not clothe me, I was sick and in prison [unjustly] and you did not look after me."
>
> They also will answer, "Lord, when did we see you hungry or thirsty . . . ?"
>
> He will reply, "I tell you the truth, whatever you did not do for one of the least of these [brothers and sisters of mine], you did not do for me." (Matthew 25:41–45)

For many years I neglected these Scriptures and was ignorant of this calling. I thank the Lord for His gentle rebuke and for removing the scales from my eyes. One day I look forward to seeing His smile and hearing Him say, "You cared for My brothers and sisters; you cared for Me."

A BETTER POSSESSION

God is not unjust; he will not forget your work and the love you have shown him as you have helped his people and continue to help them. (Hebrews 6:10)

The writer to the Hebrews affirmed a full equivalency between the readers' physical ministry to the Lord's people and directly loving the Lord Himself.

We further understand the writer's meaning when we grasp that he was writing during a time of severe persecution. He was extolling his readers for loving the Lord, specifically through their ministry to persecuted Christians. Believers lived in fear for their lives, and many of them stopped meeting together because it was dangerous to be seen associating with other Christians (10:25). Those who ministered to persecuted believers showed their love for the Lord and His children by risking their lives to help suffering saints.

You endured a great conflict of sufferings, partly by being made a public spectacle through reproaches and tribulations, and partly by becoming sharers with those who were so treated. For you showed sympathy to the prisoners and accepted joyfully the seizure of your property, knowing that you have for yourselves a better possession and a lasting one. (10:32–34, NASB)

Christians who were caught helping their suffering brothers and sisters had their property confiscated. Many believers were imprisoned during this time and were in need of daily food and clothing, because first-century prisons did not provide prisoners with life-sustaining necessities. The persecuted saints were dependent on their brothers who enjoyed liberty to bring them these things—and their brothers didn't let them down. The early church members loved Jesus and one another so much that they knowingly incriminated themselves by publicly visiting the imprisoned saints and bringing them food, water and clothing.

The writer to the Hebrews referred again to his readers' dire straits in his closing remarks:

> Let love of the brethren continue. Do not neglect to show hospitality to strangers, for by this some have entertained angels without knowing it. Remember the prisoners, as though in prison with them, and those who are ill-treated, since you yourselves also are in the body. (13:1–3, NASB)

When reading this, remember the thousands of Christian refugees described in Acts 8:1, and multiply the picture many times over in the following decades, before this letter was written. A massive number of Jesus' followers were forced on short notice to leave behind homes, possessions, livelihoods and friends. Early believers everywhere were commanded to risk everything in order to care for these homeless and imprisoned brothers and sisters. Obedience to Jesus' new command was perilous work that separated true worshippers from hypocrites.

So what should be our attitude—we who face no such danger and have been entrusted with abundance and influence—when we become aware of the basic needs of our family members around the world?

FOR THOUGHT AND DISCUSSION

Picture Jesus standing before you in the flesh, destitute, starving, thirsty and mistreated. What are you willing to do for Him?

Journaling space provided at the end of this book.

REAL LIFE IN NORTH KOREA

Sentenced Before Birth

Shin Dong-hyuk was born in 1982 in Camp 14—an internment camp for the political enemies of North Korea. Judged guilty before his conception, Shin inherited a life sentence. His parents were two hard-working prisoners rewarded with an occasional night together. Shin never felt close to either of them; his father lived and worked in another part of the megalopolis-sized camp (thirty miles long and fifteen miles wide), and his mother was just another competitor for insufficient food rations. Sometimes Shin would steal his mother's food; she would beat him with a shovel. He considered the gain to be worth its price.

For more than two decades, Shin knew of no other existence outside the camp. As far as he knew, every human alive endured the camp's day-to-day scramble for survival—every human except the all-powerful prison guards, of course. He thought it was normal to live on the edge of starvation, to labor beyond the point of exhaustion, to daily witness—and sometimes suffer—the guards' arbitrary judgments and punishments. Death was a common occurrence. He saw dozens of executions in any given year, as well as numerous deaths from starvation, disease, torture and work accidents. He assumed from near-infancy that avoiding death himself meant feeding on rats and ratting out other prisoners for rewards.

Shin saw no reason to argue when his teacher, a prison guard, explained that he and the other inmates were animals whose parents should have been killed; he believed it fully. The young prisoners learned they were paying for their parents' sins.

Shin considered it nothing unusual when a seven-year-old classmate, caught with five kernels of corn in her pocket, was beaten on the head until she collapsed. Shin helped carry her home. She died that night.

One of the most anticipated breaks from the six- or seven-day school weeks was when their teacher would, on some Saturdays, allow them to spend an hour picking lice from each other's heads.

At age thirteen, Shin turned in his mother and brother for discussing an escape attempt. He bargained with his school's night guard for a reward, but the night guard took credit for the discovery and Shin was tortured for several days in efforts to extract information. This, however, made its own kind of sense in the logic of Shin's world. After all, for several decades—including all of Shin's lifetime—it has been North Korean policy to punish not only the perpetrators of political crimes but also their family to three generations. Shin's punishment included being broiled over flames, being left hanging upside down and having his groin pierced with a steel hook to keep him from struggling. When it was learned that Shin was indeed the dutiful informant, his reward was seven months' confinement with an elderly prisoner he came to call "Uncle," who nursed Shin back from near death. Immediately upon his release, Shin was forced to witness his mother's and brother's executions—by hanging and by firing squad, respectively. At the time he thought they deserved their fates—which he knew, and still knows today, he brought about himself.

Released back into the camp population, Shin later labored in a garment factory, where he once had part of his middle finger chopped off for dropping a sewing machine. But he continued to work faithfully, in hopes that some healthy female worker might be chosen and partnered with him, as had been done for Shin's parents. His country needed him to sire strong new workers like Shin himself. Such is the circle of life at Camp 14.

When Shin met Park—a forty-some-year-old prisoner who had traveled outside North Korea—and heard the other man's stories of the outside world, he at first refused to believe such fantasies. Eventually he became convinced of their truth, and the two friends tried to escape.

Park was killed in the attempt, but at age twenty-three, Shin caught his first glimpse of the rest of the real world—the bleak terrain of wintertime North Korea. It was heaven to him.

Through China, Shin escaped to South Korea and the West. His story is one of very few to emerge through the tightly held borders of North Korea.

When Shin tells his story, observers report that he speaks "with extraordinary dignity and lack of bitterness." Why? Perhaps he has worked hard to forgive his oppressors, and this has brought him peace of mind. But probably his matter-of-factness is largely due to a deep emotional numbness. Shin has been desensitized to treatment that you and I know to be horrifically inhumane; he's conditioned to shut down emotionally when confronted with the unthinkable. He now knows intellectually that he was horribly wronged, but his ability to respond with normal emotions to his own tragedy may be impaired for life by his trauma. In his own words, "I think I am still evolving—from an animal to a human."

At one point, Shin learned that his father was originally imprisoned because his two brothers fled south during the Korean War. Shin's mother never spoke of the reasons for her presence in Camp 14, and Shin never asked.

We know that more than one in every two hundred North Koreans lives in one of these camps and expects to stay there for life. We know that more than a third of these 150,000 to 200,000 political prisoners are Christians. About a fourth of all North Korean Christians will live their entire lives in a prison camp because they, their parents or even their grandparents loved Jesus.

Imagine young Shin Dong-hyuk's story multiplied 60,000 times in the day-to-day lives of imprisoned Jesus followers. Picture yourself wanting nothing more than to live your simple life for your Lord—and as a consequence, living permanently in Camp 14, where Christians are reportedly treated even worse than other prisoners.

For the "free" three-fourths of North Korea's Christians, life isn't much happier. The dictatorship's policy gives the first fruits of its meager, mismanaged food supply to the military, leaving others to fend for themselves. The worst months are March, April and May, after the stored winter supplies have run out and before new crops begin producing. During this season, North Korea's citizens resort to eating grass and catching frogs for protein.

While enduring this "normal" lifestyle, Christians must also keep every aspect of their faith carefully hidden; worshipping God is treason, the worst of political threats to the governing regime. The country's personality cult allows only the deified Kim family to be worshipped. Children are required to learn, as their first phrase, "Thank you, Father Kim Il-sung" in reverence for communist North Korea's first dictator, the grandfather of current dictator Kim Jong-un. Failure to precede any of the three Kims' names with "Great Leader" is a crime punishable by incarceration of one's entire family.

It has become evident that the Kim regime is systematically exterminating Christians. The four officially sanctioned "churches" in the capital city of Pyongyang—two Protestant, one Catholic and one Orthodox—serve only as showpieces to the outside world and to lure hidden Christians into the open. Whenever true believers in Jesus are discovered—often by spies who infiltrate the churches and gain their trust—they're dealt with summarily and fatally.

One small underground church was uncovered when the North Korean army demolished a vacant house to widen a highway. In the basement, between two bricks, soldiers found a Bible and a list of twenty-five names—the pastor, two assistant pastors, two elders and twenty other members.

The military police hunted down every individual on the list and detained them without trial. Later that month they herded the small congregation back to the road construction site where an audience had been gathered and seated. The five church leaders were bound hand and foot and made to lie on the ground in front of a steamroller. They were ordered to deny their faith and pledge their devotion only to Kim Jong-il and his father, Kim Il-sung. After the church leaders remained silent, their twenty followers and the rest of the assembled audience watched the steamroller drive over the clergy. The popping of their skulls caused observers to scream and faint.

What of the other twenty Christians? They were destined for the existence of Shin Dong-hyuk and his parents, perhaps even in Camp 14. A few of these brothers and sisters may still survive, silently praising their Lord, thanking Him for His daily provision of snakes, rats and undigested corn kernels dug out of cow dung.[13]

CHAPTER 7

Acceptable Worship

What is worship? According to the Bible, our worship must include more than what we do in our church services if it is to be pleasing and acceptable to the Lord. And, as we're about to see, caring for suffering Christians is one of the most pleasant and fragrant of worship offerings.

We've seen that the writer to the Hebrews gave us a strong exhortation to "show hospitality to strangers" and to "remember those in prison . . . and those who are mistreated" (Hebrews 13:2–3). If we look back just a couple of verses from there, we see that these specific actions are biblical expressions of acceptable worship (Hebrews 12:28). The author is telling us to worship the Lord with reverence and awe—by caring for persecuted and suffering saints. The apostle Paul was passionate about supporting suffering and persecuted believers. Paul's passion was rooted in his understanding of worship. Consider Paul's instruction in Romans 12:1:

> I urge you, brethren, by the mercies of God, to present your bodies a living and holy sacrifice, acceptable to God, which is your spiritual service of worship. (NASB)

Apparently not all worship is acceptable to the Lord. Notice the verses following Romans 12:1, where Paul provided examples of acceptable worship: "Contributing to the needs of others . . . give generously. . . . Be devoted to one another in brotherly love. . . . Share with God's people who are in need. Practice hospitality" (12:8,10,13).

According to Paul, contributing to the needs of the saints is an acceptable sacrifice of worship. What's more, Paul's very example underscored the global nature of this responsibility. He wrote the letter to the Romans, including the words we just read, while carrying a generous relief gift from the believers in Macedonia and Achaia (in modern Greece) to the suffering Christians in Judea (see Romans 15:25–26). This was a thousand-mile journey that required months and many perils. The barriers between the Macedonian and Achaian believers and their Judean brothers and sisters were far greater in their day than the barriers between us and anyone else in our world. But these Christians didn't balk at reaching out in a significant, tangible way to fellow believers in need.

The Macedonian believers exemplified acceptable, fragrant worship. They were suffering their own financial hardships, yet they were more than willing to help suffering believers in Jesus. Paul boasted about their amazing worship:

> Out of . . . their extreme poverty . . . they gave as much as they were able, and even beyond their ability . . . in this service to the saints. (2 Corinthians 8:2–4)

THE PRIVILEGE OF SHARING

Paul's church plants demonstrated a supernatural unity and sacrificial love for one another—even when the givers themselves were suffering persecution. This begs the question: What did Paul believe? And what was he teaching his converts to cause them to give "even beyond their ability" to help suffering Christians in a foreign land—people they would never meet in their lifetimes?

We discover some of Paul's foundational convictions in the letter he wrote to churches in Galatia. Here Paul reported an important visit he paid to the church leaders in Jerusalem:

> James, Peter and John, those reputed to be pillars, gave me and Barnabas the right hand of fellowship when they recognized the grace given to me. They agreed that we should go to the Gentiles, and they to the Jews. All they asked was that we should continue to remember the poor, the very thing I was eager to do. (Galatians 2:9–10)

Paul's calling was to carry the light of the gospel to the Gentiles. However, his ministry was also defined by his passionate and persistent advocacy and fundraising for the poor, suffering and persecuted believers. Peter, James and John—back at Jerusalem Central—were so emphatic that ministry to the suffering saints should be a priority that they conditioned their blessing of Paul's mission on his fulfilling of this responsibility, alongside his evangelism. But the needs of his suffering brothers and sisters were already heavy on Paul's heart.

Later in this same letter, Paul clarified the believer's obligation to care for all people. But he also made it unmistakably clear that the highest priority was to care for fellow Christians (Galatians 6:10). Paul taught and supported this priority throughout his ministry.

In Paul's first letter to the believers at Corinth (in Achaia), we see that he was collecting money on behalf of suffering and persecuted saints:

> Now concerning the collection for the saints, as I have given orders to the churches of Galatia, so you must do also: On the first day of the week let each one of you lay something aside, storing up as he may prosper, that there be no collections when I come. (1 Corinthians 16:1–2, NKJV)

This is the only reference to Sunday offerings in the New Testament; the purpose of these offerings was explicitly for the benefit of suffering believers in a foreign land. These were not optional; Paul required the Corinthians to give.

By the time Paul wrote his second letter to the Corinthians, his advocacy for the persecuted had proven so successful that he could say, "The ministry of this service is . . . *fully* supplying the needs of the saints" in Judea (2 Corinthians 9:12, NASB). These were more than mere token offerings; they were substantial gifts that allowed complete relief for thousands of refugees from Jerusalem.

CONTEXT IS CRITICAL

Second Corinthians 8–9 is a treasure trove of biblical principles about giving that you have probably read or heard taught many times. I encourage you to read these passages again, staying mindful of how Paul issued these teachings in the context of contributing specifically to the needs of suffering and persecuted Christians.

Among the truth-nuggets in this treatise is the aptly named "Law of the Harvest":

> Whoever sows sparingly will also reap sparingly, and whoever sows generously will also reap generously. (2 Corinthians 9:6)

This teaching has a variety of valid applications, but we miss Paul's central meaning if we forget that he was referring to supporting suffering Christians. We could paraphrase it, "The Lord will sparingly reward those who sparingly support their suffering brothers and sisters; and the Lord will generously reward those who generously give to the needs of suffering believers in Christ." Take a moment to consider this amazing promise as it was originally intended. The Lord, who created and controls everything, will generously reward the one who shares with persecuted believers in Jesus.

Recall, as we saw earlier, that Paul exhorted the Corinthians to "excel in this grace of giving" to suffering brothers and sisters (2 Corinthians 8:7). In this context, Paul also explained that we *prove* our confession of the gospel and our love for one another by generously supporting the suffering saints:

> *Openly before the churches, show them the proof of your love* and of our reason for boasting about you. . . . Because of the *proof* given by this ministry, they will glorify God for your obedience to your confession of the gospel of Christ and for the liberality of your contribution to them and to all. (2 Corinthians 8:24; 9:13, NASB)

Words come easily. "We love God and we love people," say millions of Christians. But where's the proof? How can others tell that these claims are true? Paul says we prove it by caring for suffering brothers and sisters around the world. Our support for the suffering saints should be a natural and inextricable outflow of our confession of the gospel. It's unnatural to profess Christ while not caring for persecuted coconfessors.

Paul commands us to do this "openly before the [other] churches." As I've explained, very few American Christians are aware of—let alone focused on—ministering to the needs of persecuted Christians. This must change. And the change must start somewhere. Will it start with you and your church? Will you show the proof of your love in acceptable worship by elevating "this grace of giving" for the persecuted to the level of importance and priority the Lord requires? And will you humbly allow your conviction and follow-through to be known in the Christian community, so that others might be stirred and challenged by your example?

Light will overcome the darkness as we show the proof of our love. Lives will be changed and our brothers and sisters in other parts of the world will "glorify God for [our] obedience to [our] confession of the gospel of Christ."

FOR THOUGHT AND DISCUSSION

In eternity, when you meet the Macedonian family—the parents, the children—who gave up regular meals in order to help brothers and sisters suffering in Judea, will you tell them how their examples prodded you toward sacrificial generosity to believers in Laos, Eritrea, Pakistan, or other places of oppression? Or will you lower your eyes in shame, knowing they gave out of their poverty and you held onto your abundance?

Journaling space provided at the end of this book.

Twenty-First-Century Holocaust

"Let me show you something. See for yourself." Marriam Teia leads us deeper into her dirt-floored cave home in the southern Nuba Mountains of Sudan. "This is the last sack for the kids. Just that small sack." Her work-toughened hand pats a roughly gallon-sized volume of food grain—probably sorghum—inside the bag.

We're watching Marriam via an online video.[14] Two unidentified children tag along with her, gazing curiously at the camera. After displaying her family's remaining food supply, Marriam looks back at the camera. We don't see overt fear or worry on her face—just a blankness due to exhaustion from a lifestyle of daily trauma. Marriam must conserve the energy she would otherwise expend in emotional expression. But you can be sure she harbors the anxiety, the terror, inside.

"This won't even last us ten days," she explains. "And when it is finished we will be worn out with nothing to give these children." She picks up an empty bucket-like container with a trace of ground grain left in the bottom. "Nothing to be eaten. This is the core issue affecting us."

Why are Marriam and her children living in a mountain cave on a bare survival diet? Because her own government is purposefully, systematically eradicating her people—the Nuba—as well as virtually all other non-Arab peoples remaining in Sudan.

It's nothing new. When genocidal dictator Omar al-Bashir seized power in 1989, he immediately began his campaign of extermination. Twenty-seven years and more than two million dead Jesus followers later, the world's leaders are still yawning and idly watching. Meanwhile, Bashir continues in his holocaust-like crimes against his own people, in full view of the world.

The International Criminal Court has indicted him on three counts of genocide, five counts of crimes against humanity (murder, extermination, forcible transfer, torture and rape) and two counts of war crimes (pillaging and intentionally directing attacks against civilians). Bashir considers virtually all indigenous Africans (black Africans, as opposed to Arabs) to be Christians. Throughout his nearly three decades in power he has attempted to force every Sudanese citizen to become both Muslim by faith and Arab by culture and language. He wants a "pure" Muslim nation, which in his thinking means a purely Arab nation. Any who resist must die. Those who simply want to go about their daily lives—planting their fields, plying their crafts, caring for their families—are perceived as resisting and presenting a "threat" to Bashir's regime.

That's why Tess, Marriam's home village, was attacked by government troops. That's why Marriam found herself suddenly a widow, her husband shot and killed in the attack. That's why Marriam fled with her children and her sister, along with a few hundred thousand others, to the mountain caves or across the border. That's why government and mercenary soldiers continue to terrorize "Christian" regions in Sudan by means of aerial bombing and forced mass starvation. The daily bombings keep terrified families from raising their subsistence crops or venturing out for clean drinking water.

The Bashir regime is content to wait. They'll wait until Marriam and her children die of starvation, thirst or disease. Bashir doesn't care which takes them. A dead Nuban, by whatever means, is no less dead.

Forces inside and outside Sudan have spoken up for the rights of these oppressed people. Time after time, Bashir and his representatives have given verbal promises and signed agreements and treaties. Then they've walked away from each agreement secretly laughing at the gullibility of these would-be rescuers.

The current mass starvation campaign against the Nuba began on June 5, 2011, and is still ongoing at the time of this writing. Five growing seasons have seen fallow fields. Five rainy seasons have come and gone, but the rain has found no newly planted crops to nurture. Five years have passed and the starving Nuban men, women and children have waited in their caves for help. Only Bashir's bombs come their way. He has blocked all humanitarian aid to their region.

"No food, no water," says Marriam. "Do you see what our situation looks like? We are drinking water from that hole." In the video we see a few seconds of what looks to be chocolate milk pouring from a plastic container into a pot. It's the purest water available.

"They poison us. They leave us without water to make food for the children. Nothing to be given to the elderly mother and father. It is painful."

All that these people possess is whatever they grabbed when they fled their homes, combined with the meager offerings of the land within running distance of the caves. When Marriam's precious bag of grain is empty, she will have the children digging in the dry, packed soil for roots and climbing the few trees for their leaves—foods that provide little or no nutritional value.

"They come and kill the children, hit us with bombs. . . . The real problem is the [bomber plane] that comes to kill our children. [It comes to kill] your mother, your brother and even you. For the government to come and kill its own people here, that is unacceptable to me."

For some of the afflicted, the answer is Yida—the name of a village and its overflowing refugee camp just across the border in the relative safety of independent South Sudan. The camp was originally meant for fifteen thousand refugees, but at last report the actual population was nearing one hundred thousand. The several-day journey is perilous; one documented group set out for the camp with 1700 refugees, was attacked along the way, and arrived with only seven hundred survivors. Since the independence of South Sudan, Bashir's planes have even crossed the border and bombed the camp. The butcher doesn't just want the Nuba people to leave. He wants them dead.

Marriam has considered the several-day trek to Yida with her children. "Right now I don't know where to put my heart," she says. "I am in the middle. I don't know if I should go back to Tess, or should I go to Yida?" She ponders the unfamiliar, the frighteningly strange. "I have never seen Yida before. There are no means to get us from here to there." And she ponders her familiar home; should she wait out the bombings and hope for a chance to return and rebuild? "I want to return, but the enemy burned our possessions, and destroyed our land. That is what is keeping us here."

In a closing scene we see Marriam's face—the drawn face of a woman who has already shed a lifetime of tears. "We need the world to come and save us from these problems. That is what we wish for."

The world? She's talking about you and me.[15]

CHAPTER 8

Above All Else

The freedom and prosperity that we enjoy here in the West makes it difficult for us to comprehend heirloom love. We have to work at grasping the mindset and assumptions with which much of the New Testament was written.

The early church was born and grew in a context of persecution. During the first century, the pre-believer considering faith in Jesus Christ had to weigh the likely cost. He or she might face rejection from family and friends, boycotting by customers or clients (if not complete loss of livelihood), loss of home and possessions, wrongful lawsuits and imprisonment, and possible torture and death at the hands of authorities or other hostile parties. Certainly there were pockets of Christians here and there who experienced peace and security for limited periods. But as a rule, to be a Christian in the first century was to face the troubles that Jesus predicted for us. When we read and interpret New Testament statements without acknowledging this context of danger, hostility and near-universal suffering and loss, we're likely to miss critical aspects of the meaning of the teachings—often the primary meaning.

PETER'S PRIORITIES

Peter wrote to a persecuted and suffering people. He mentioned their suffering in every chapter of his first letter. In his greeting, he referred to them as "strangers in the world, scattered"—as refugees—throughout several large regions in Asia Minor (modern Turkey; 1 Peter 1:1). They "had to suffer grief in all kinds of trials" (1:6). And why were they suffering? Often "for doing good" as Jesus' followers (2:20; 3:17). Peter urged them to follow the example of Jesus in suffering (3:21–25; 4:1). And he wrote to them:

> Dear friends, do not be surprised at the painful trial you are suffering, as though something strange were happening to you. But rejoice that you participate in the sufferings of Christ, so that you may be overjoyed when his glory is revealed. (4:12–13)

> Those who suffer according to God's will should commit themselves to their faithful Creator and continue to do good. (4:19)

> You know that your brothers throughout the world are undergoing the same kind of sufferings. And the God of all grace, who called you to his eternal glory in Christ, after you have suffered a little while, will himself restore you and make you strong, firm and steadfast. (5:9–10)

It's in this persecution context that Peter wrote one of the key passages for this book: "*Above all things* have fervent love *[agapē]* for one another" (1 Peter 4:8, NKJV).

This statement is rooted in the authentic heirloom love we're trying to recover. Love for fellow believers is an ongoing theme throughout Peter's letter; just as he mentioned his readers' suffering in every chapter, so also in every chapter he exhorted them to love each other (1:22; 2:17; 3:8; 4:8; 5:14). Peter would never deny the importance of loving unbelievers; after all, he walked beside the Master Himself and watched Jesus loving every type of person He encountered. But again we see a priority on showing love toward each other within the worldwide body of Christ.

By using the phrase "above all things," Peter stressed that the command to love each other stands as the highest priority. I'm sure Peter considered all his teachings to be important, but like Paul (see Colossians 3:14), he didn't hesitate to proclaim a hierarchy among the Bible's teachings. And at the top of the list is—what else?—Jesus' new command. I believe Peter would agree with this paraphrase: "If you remember nothing else I've written, remember and obey this: Love each other." In the context of Peter's letter, this highest of all priorities had to naturally include generous expressions of love toward the practical needs of persecuted and suffering fellow believers.

Peter's priority—*above all else* to love the saints, especially by caring for those in suffering and persecution—rocked my spiritual world. For years I lived with a complacent conception of these commands. More than anything else I share in this book, 1 Peter 4:8 was my wakeup call to what the Lord requires of me. The Lord is using this command and its implications to overcome my lazy, selfish and apathetic inclinations. The implications of this command are significant and I'm still in the early stages of grasping how it affects my worldview and my life purpose and priorities.

Finally, Peter commanded that this love toward one another be "fervent." The Greek word Peter used is *ektenēs,* which means that our love, including our support for the suffering saints, should be vigilant, unrelenting, continual, persevering. Our calling and duty to show unconditional, tangible, unceasing love toward each other—especially toward saints in tribulation—is an intense, twenty-four-seven responsibility.

Please pray with me that the Lord would fill us with a holy zeal to spend *ourselves*—not just our money—in persistent pursuit of Him by loving His persecuted children.

JAMES DEFINES TRUE RELIGION

From the first verse of his letter, James evidenced his mindfulness of his persecuted readership. James addressed the letter "to the twelve tribes scattered among the nations" (James 1:1)—a clear reference to the dispersion of Jewish Christian refugees who had fled their homes to escape the "great persecution" (see Acts 8:1; 11:19).

Before the end of the letter's first chapter, we come to a well-known passage that begins, "Do not merely listen to the word, and so deceive yourselves. Do what it says" (1:22). Then notice what James taught as the pinnacle of such obedience:

> Pure and genuine religion in the sight of God the Father means caring for orphans and widows in their distress and refusing to let the world corrupt you. (1:27, NLT)

James was echoing an often mentioned litmus test for the faithfulness of God's people in the Old Testament—whether they helped care for widows and orphans (see, for example, Isaiah 1:16–17; 58:6–7). The new factor for James's New Testament readership was that many of the "widows and orphans in their distress" were families of martyred Christians. This ultimate test of "pure and genuine religion in the sight of God the Father" boiled down, in many cases, to caring for victims of persecution. What's more, in verse 27 James asserted that caring for the widows and orphans of the martyred saints is as fundamental and essential to genuine Christian faith as keeping ourselves from being corrupted by the world.

James next addressed favoritism toward the rich over the poor. Many of these poor would have become so when they fled persecution and left behind their possessions and livelihoods (2:1–13).

He then launched into the nature of genuine faith (as opposed to "faith" in name only):

> What good is it, my brothers, if a man claims to have faith but has no deeds? Can such faith save him? Suppose a brother or sister is without clothes and daily food. If one of you says to him, "Go, I wish you well; keep warm and well fed," but does nothing about his physical needs, what good is it? In the same way, faith by itself, if it is not accompanied by action, is dead. (2:14–17)

James's argument continues through verse 26, but these opening verses are enough here to make the point: To illustrate the expression of genuine faith, James cited the believer who provides clothing and daily food to fellow believers who are so poor they have neither. Whether this condition was due to persecution or some other cause, the fact remains that many believers among James's readers were absolutely destitute, and he could think of no better expression of genuine faith than to provide for such needs within the family of faith.

The essence of James's message through most of chapters 1 and 2 is that ministering to desperately needy Christians is the substance and evidence of genuine faith. James boldly stated that we're deluded—he even questioned whether we're truly saved—if we don't show mercy to suffering and persecuted Christians by providing for their physical needs.

Since starting our journey into heirloom love, my family has financially participated in a number of relief projects for persecuted believers. Each of these has been special and uniquely rewarding, but one project stands out as perhaps more gratifying than the others. A season of widespread rioting and Christian persecution throughout a large Asian city culminated with the brutal beatings and murders of dozens of pastors and church leaders—some even set afire in front of their families. In the aftermath, we were able to financially help the suddenly orphaned children and widows of those brave and faithful men. The money went toward relocating these desperate families to safety in other cities, prepaying their rent, providing the widows with training and the means to start home-based businesses, and introducing them to new local churches that would care for them. Although I have never met these grieving families, I am deeply thankful for the opportunity to help them. And I have joyful anticipation of meeting them in heaven.

Many organizations do great work reaching out to widows and orphans around the world, but very few seem to give proper biblical weight and priority to the families of the martyred saints. Consequently we tend to neglect the widows and orphans of our murdered brothers and sisters. At most we give them no more attention than the rest of the world's needy. This may seem "fair," but it's not biblical.

JOHN AND THE BELIEVER'S BIRTHMARK

Near the end of the first century, when John wrote his epistles, Christianity had been around long enough that false teachers had arisen—those who had figured out how to use the name of Christ for personal gain. They mixed enough truth to draw would-be Jesus followers astray with enough falsehood to keep the followers from salvation and eternity.

That's why John wrote his first epistle: specifically to dispel false teachings and to help us know whether we've truly been born again to eternal life.

These things I have written to you concerning those who are trying to deceive you. . . . These things I have written to you who believe in the name of the Son of God, so that you may know that you have eternal life. (1 John 2:26; 5:13, NASB)

John's doctrine on how we can know we have eternal life can be summarized in the following verses.

We know that we have passed from death to life, because we love our brothers. Anyone who does not love remains in death. . . . If anyone has material possessions and sees his brother in need but has no pity on him, how can the love of God be in him? Dear children, let us not love with words or tongue but with actions and in truth. This then is how we know that we belong to the truth. (3:14,17–19)

Doesn't this sound amazingly similar to James's tests of genuine faith? Once again we see that the tangible expression of love toward fellow believers is the ultimate test of true faith.

Almost 40 percent of the verses in John's letter on authentic Christianity (39 out of 105 total) pertain to obedience to Jesus' new command to love all the saints. In John's terminology our sacrificial love for fellow believers is like a birthmark that provides visible evidence of our rebirth and validates the authenticity of our faith. This birthmark is our assurance that we've truly passed out of death and into life. It is the same mark Jesus said would reveal to the world that we're His true disciples (see John 13:34–35).

John was so confident in the inseparable nature of *agapē* love and true faith that he boldly said,

> This is how we know who the children of God are and who the children of the devil are: Anyone who does not do what is right is not God's child, nor is anyone who does not love their brother and sister. (1 John 3:10, NIV-2011)

Refusing to share our material possessions with our needy brothers and sisters is equivalent to hate. Using John's logic, we either *agapē* love or we hate—there is no middle ground. And those who hate, according to John, are murderers (3:15) and therefore children of the devil.

John allowed for imperfection in the believer's conduct (see 1:8–2:1) as long as the primary characteristics of one's conduct are doing what is right and loving one's brother. During the years when I lived in ignorance of Christian persecution and the New Testament mandate to love, I was still a believer in Jesus. I was saved. My thinking and behavior was characteristically godly and right in many ways. The same is true for many believers in Jesus today; they may still be in the process of learning to walk in truth, or they've lost their first love and need to repent. These shortcomings alone do not make them "children of the devil."

Still, John used stark language to teach and warn us against being deceived in this most important matter. He said in no uncertain terms that those who do not characteristically express *agapē* love toward fellow believers are children of the devil.

Saving belief in Jesus is inseparable from obedience to Jesus' new command. The two are so closely interrelated that John referred to them as one command:

This is his command: to believe in the name of his Son, Jesus Christ, and to love one another as he commanded us. (3:23)

Caring for family is simply something that family does.

FOR THOUGHT AND DISCUSSION

Take a few minutes and meditate on 1 Peter 4:8. How does Peter's emphasis on loving needy fellow believers "above all" compare with your current priorities?

- *Honestly, how do you respond when you read John's black-and-white statements about who does and does not belong to Christ? Are they prompting you to change something in your relationship with the Lord or in how you use your time, energy, money and possessions?*

- *Why might Christians resist placing a biblical emphasis and priority on helping persecuted believers in Jesus? For each reason you think of, how would James (or other New Testament writers) respond?*

Journaling space provided at the end of this book.

REAL LIFE IN SYRIA

Disposable People

To stay or to go? Either choice might mean death to Christians in war-torn Syria. Either way, these precious brothers and sisters—women, men and children made in God's image, who choose to worship their Creator and Savior—are treated like roaches scuttling underfoot by those who carelessly control their destinies.

Pastor Ouseph (not his real name) has chosen to stay. He, his wife, Hanna, and his two young daughters have refused to flee their home and church in Damascus, in spite of the dangers from both sides of the Syrian civil war.

Before March 2011, Syria was one of the safest places in the Middle East for Christians; Ouseph and his people enjoyed a significant degree of religious freedom under President Bashar al-Assad. But that changed when war broke out, especially with the inflow of foreign Muslim combatants, including ISIS, among the opposition forces, bringing with them their disdain for Christians.

The conflict is essentially Muslim against Muslim, with Syria's two million Christians—about 10 percent of the population—

caught in the crossfire. Whole cities have been devastated. The rebels—who accuse Christians of siding with the Assad government—have held scores of Christians as human shields against undeterred government forces; both sides fight on, heedless of the countless innocent lives they squash. Neither side is seriously bothered by the "collateral damage," especially if it involves the likes of Ouseph.

In the five years of war at the time of this writing, between 220,000 and 380,000 have died, including nearly 14,000 children. Nearly five million Syrians—more than half of them children—have fled their country, with Christians a significant portion of these. Another six to seven million are displaced and homeless within the country, and an estimated thirteen to fourteen million—four-fifths of the remaining population—lack food and other survival basics.

Increasingly, Christians like Ouseph are being targeted for kidnapping or detention, rape, torture and murder. Both government and opposition forces are committing these atrocities, as are criminal networks that operate unchecked. Both sides of the conflict use suicide bombers, which kill as many civilians as military targets. And both sides have tortured children, including infants.

Here in the West, when we tuck our children into bed, we don't have to prepare them for missiles coming through the ceiling, the way Pastor Ouseph does with his girls: "If a bomb explodes, you might see a lot of blood, and it might hurt a little, but if we die, we will close our eyes here and reopen them in heaven."

When our kids arrive at school, they don't have to check the trash bins for bombs every morning. "God has saved us many times by showing us the location of bombs so they could be disarmed," explains Hanna.

In fact, Ouseph's and Hanna's children are fortunate. Many schools throughout Syria are closed. Children are being deprived of the education that would otherwise provide the foundation of a successful adult life. Instead their real-world "education" involves the routine trauma of mortar shelling and the random threat of sniper fire. Ouseph himself can show you the hole in each of his suits, from a bullet that passed through their home while the family was away.

Why do they stay? The answer is rooted in the conviction of Ouseph's family, together with a dwindling number of remaining Syrian Christians, that this land is not only their home but also a part of the dark world that needs the Lord's light. They feel a sense of mission. Their culture might treat them as disposable, but they know better. They remain steadfastly obedient to their calling to perpetuate the Christian presence in Syria, which goes back to the first century. The apostle Paul found Christ on the road to Damascus, and in that Syrian capital it's still possible to walk Straight Street where Ananias baptized Paul.

Ouseph, Hanna and the girls know that if the darkness succeeds in driving out Christians, then only darkness will govern this land. They are the light. "If there is no earthly thing to trust in, you have to trust in God, and this is what He teaches us to do through this difficult situation," Ouseph explains. Even now, in the midst of daily peril, they and other Christians are reaching out in the name of Jesus and expanding Christ's kingdom in Syria. Muslim women, whose husbands have gone off to war, have begun to come to Ouseph's church to learn about Jesus and His good news of freedom and life.

The believers at this church have also been praying and fasting on behalf of Christians in the city of Homs, a hundred miles to the north. Homs has been virtually obliterated by bombings, and many of the Homs believers have escaped to Damascus, into the care of Ouseph's church family. "God . . . sent the people of Homs to our church, and the revival is happening right here," says Ouseph. "They renewed their faith in the midst of crisis." These refugees have lost everything—jobs, schools, homes, possessions, all sense of normalcy. But they, like Ouseph and his family, are learning to see God's eternal, otherworldly blessings even more clearly than the earthly blessings they've lost. And they're learning to bless the name of the Lord, even when He takes away.

These are the reasons Ouseph and his family remain in Syria. In Hanna's words, "It's important the church stays in Syria. If the church leaves Syria, Syria will be spiritually destroyed."

Ouseph adds, "God has saved us so far, so we are still needed. If we keep praying, God will do something incredible. This is what we all feel."

In contrast, Jacob's family came to the conclusion that they had no choice but to send him out of Syria—a course of action fraught with its own huge risks.

Jacob was a university student studying economics, on track for a life of relative success and privilege. But the incidence of kidnapping and killing of Christians had risen to the point that he dared not continue attending. However, once Jacob stopped attending the university, he was no longer exempt from compulsory military service. To Jacob and his family this was a double-threat: Not only would it place Jacob in mortal danger—two of his friends had already died in battle—but engaging in violence is contrary to their Christian convictions. Jacob would be forced to violate his conscience.

When police abusively harassed and detained Jacob for his failure to enlist, the family knew it was only a matter of time before he would be either conscripted or imprisoned as a deserter and possibly executed. They paid seventeen thousand dollars to smuggle Jacob out of the country—eventually, they hoped, to a growing Syrian community in Sweden. They knew that human traffickers are notoriously unreliable and that many of the people they transport end up sold into slavery, abandoned to die in shipping containers or boat cargo holds, or sometimes deported back to Syria by foreign governments. But despite their misgivings, they placed Jacob in the hands of strangers.

In the dark hours one morning, Jacob was surprised to learn he was to leave immediately. He bade his mother and three younger brothers a tearful goodbye; they might never see each other again.

In a succession of always-crowded minivans and cars, Jacob was transported into Turkey, through Istanbul, and ultimately into a Turkish forest, where he and his fellow refugees followed a fifteen-year-old boy on foot for eight hours. They used inflatable boats to cross a waterway into Greece, where the Greek border police found them. Fortunately the police treated the refugees kindly, giving them some type of identification as refugees and informing them that they needed to leave the country within ten days. Jacob and the others made their own way to Athens by bus, where they were met by new Syrian smugglers. Jacob was kept for nearly two months in a single room with twenty men; they were so crowded that they took shifts sleeping on the floor.

Several times Jacob was supplied with passports of different nationalities and attempted to leave Athens by plane, but he was repeatedly turned away. He was finally threatened with deportation to Syria if he returned to the airport.

Jacob was eventually smuggled out of Greece in a small boat's cargo hold. He was promised he would be one of five, but he ended up crammed into the airless hold—at gunpoint—with seventy men, women and children. That began their "four-hour journey," which turned into four days. The refugees received water once each day, were given no food, and had nowhere but the floor to vomit, urinate and defecate. Some non-Christians saw Jacob wearing a cross and attacked him and his Syrian companions, but others stepped in to protect them. Jacob's back was bloodied and his eye blackened.

On the fourth day Jacob felt a sudden jar when the boat struck an obstacle and halted. By the time the refugees broke down the cargo hold's metal door and reached the deck, the boat's crew had taken the one lifeboat and were long gone. The boat was stranded a kilometer from land, and the refugees had been abandoned like livestock.

In spite of several days without food, clean air or proper rest, Jacob and several others swam to shore, helping each other as needed. The effort completely exhausted Jacob.

Remaining on the boat were several who either could not swim or didn't have the strength to reach shore. One of them was a countryman of Jacob's, a Kurdish Muslim who screamed that he was a father and that his family was awaiting him in Switzerland.

On land, Jacob found some nuts to eat for strength. Then he found tires that he used as floatation devices. He swam with them back out to the boat, then expended the last of his strength towing the Kurdish father back to shore. Once safely ashore, says Jacob, "I asked the Muslim if he would have helped me if I had been in the same situation. He said he wouldn't have, since I am a Christian. But for the rest of his life he would never forget that I helped him and from now on he would change."

As many as thirty of the refugees drowned trying to reach shore. The forty survivors learned they'd come ashore in Italy, and within days, Jacob joined relatives in Sweden. He was emaciated—down about twenty-five pounds from his normal weight—and emotionally destroyed by the traumatic experience. Even now he needs medication to help him sleep.

It was last reported in April 2013 that Jacob was still awaiting a residency permit in Sweden and was apparently still in danger of being deported.

Whether they stay or whether they flee, Syrian Christians face danger from those who view them as nothing more than disposable commodities, and often as far less. Despite the supreme disrespect and scorn implied in the attitudes of others, our brothers and sisters insist on looking to their Creator and their Savior Jesus for their real worth. And in Him they shine. They reach out with love, touching and moving hearts wherever they go.

Let's learn from them. And when we can, let's help them.[16]

CHAPTER 9

Measuring Love: The Sincerity Test

When faced with the immense worldwide need, the lone individual always, at some point, ends up asking a valid question: How much should I give? (Or, How do I know when I'm giving my share?)

Tied directly to this is another question: What is a legitimate standard of living for my family and me? Consideration of our living standard is important because the more simply and modestly we live, the more we have available to help others.

These are difficult questions, to which I know no simple answers. And the answers for you are probably different than they are for me. Even within my own family we don't always agree. I have erred on both sides—on the side of frugality to a fault (penny-wise and pound-foolish) and, at other times, on the side of overspending and excessive consumption. Although I don't have all the answers, I can share the truths the Lord has used to guide me on the journey into heirloom love.

The Lord has provided us with a key principle to help guide our decisions about how much we keep and how much we give. It's not a way of measuring our giving, but a God-given way of measuring our hearts and our love. It's called sincerity.

LOVE WITHOUT HYPOCRISY

Love must be sincere. . . . Be devoted to one another in brotherly love. . . . Share with God's people who are in need. (Romans 12:9–10,13)

In Paul's teaching, a true expression of sincere love (12:9) includes sharing with our Christian brothers and sisters in need. In this verse the Greek word Paul used for "sincere" is *anupokritos*. It's created by connecting the prefix an- (meaning "not" or "without") with the word *hupokritēs* (from which we derive our word "hypocrite"). In fact, the NASB translates it "without hypocrisy." In ancient Greek culture, a *hupokritēs* was an actor who wore a mask on stage to represent his character. So hypocrisy is putting on an act, wearing a mask or disguise, presenting a front to hide what is underneath. And its opposite (not-hypocrisy) is open, undisguised sincerity.

Therefore, Paul teaches us that one guideline for the expression of sincere love is that it has nothing to hide. When "love" is hiding something, it holds back and does less than it is able. Paul said that "the gift is acceptable according to what one has" (2 Corinthians 8:12). Our sincerity—and the Lord's acceptance of our offering—is measured in part by our ability. If we claim to love and it is within our means to help, yet we choose to do less than we could—due to indifference or selfishness—we're hypocrites. We're hiding something.

The first disciples to be called Christians demonstrated love without hypocrisy by giving according to their ability:

The disciples were called Christians first at Antioch. . . . Each according to his ability decided to provide help for the brothers living in Judea. (Acts 11:26)

Paul presented the Macedonian church as a model for sincere obedience to Jesus' new command (see 2 Corinthians 8–9). These fellow believers passed the sincerity test—they were without hypocrisy and had nothing to hide. They so loved their needy, faraway brothers and sisters that they gave "even beyond their ability" (8:3).

LOVE WITHOUT DEFECT

Paul's prayers give us insight into some of his highest priorities and concerns for the church. The following prayer for the Christians at Philippi (one of the Macedonian cities) is especially pertinent to our topic:

> This I pray, that your love *[agapē]* may abound still more and more in real knowledge and all discernment, so that you may approve the things that are excellent, in order to be sincere and blameless until the day of Christ. (Philippians 1:9–10, NASB)

Here in the NASB we find again the word "sincere," this time translated from Paul's choice of the Greek word *eilikrinēs*. This word is a compound of *heilios* ("sun") and *krinos* ("judge, test"). It literally means "judged by sunlight" and relates to certain trades in the ancient world. For example, when a maker or buyer of pottery or fabric wanted to discern a product's quality, one way was to hold it up and allow sunlight to shine through it. This would reveal any defects in a weave or hairline cracks in baked clay. The word came to apply to anything that was somehow tested and demonstrated to be free of defects or impurities—as with gold or silver, for example, that contained no alloys.

For us to pass this test of purity or "sincerity," Paul prayed that we might "abound still more and more in real knowledge and all discernment, so that you may approve the things that are excellent." When our knowledge and discernment of truth become sullied with the world's thinking, we begin to approve and follow the world's misguided values. When we adopt even a small degree of materialistic thinking, we start to lose our ability to discern the Lord's will and begin investing our resources in things of temporal value, rather than people and causes with eternal value. Truth becomes warped, our vision becomes darkened and blurred by the world's influence. And our love becomes misguided, so that it no longer passes the sincerity test for defects. Our consumption-driven Western culture has distorted the terms "ability," "need" and "disposable income." The majority of the world's population—the portion that doesn't share in our freedom and material abundance—is more likely to be "sincere" or pure in their thinking about these terms.

Consider the following true story of a pastor and ministry I work with. The pastor, from a third-world country, was visiting the US for the first time. Many people in his country are slowly perishing due to a lack of food, medical care and other life-sustaining resources. The average life expectancy in his country for an adult male is only forty-seven years (compared to seventy-five in the US). Many of his people often go one or more days without food, and when they do eat, they typically have only one meal a day, which consists of one scoop of beans and one scoop of rice.

This pastor openly wept when he saw that we have animal hospitals, while many of his people are perishing for lack of basic medical care. He cried out to the Lord and asked if he and his people were less than human because the Lord gave animal hospitals to the American people but has withheld even the basics for life from his people.

This pastor has the real knowledge and discernment to help us see through our religious veneer, our self-justification and our cultural desensitization. He can objectively identify our blind spots, the impurities in our vision, the cracks in our love. He knows the difference between worldly "love" and true sincerity-tested love. I wonder how he would counsel us if we invited him into our homes and allowed him to review our finances and our schedules. Would I truly listen? Would you?

IN SEARCH OF SINCERE LOVE

The sincerity of our love is the measure that guides what we give and what we keep. None of us begins with perfectly sincere love; we grow and transform over time, as we conform to the likeness of the Lord Jesus Christ. Along the way we wrestle with individual choices: Is the Lord honored if we replace our car or buy a boat or update our clothes? For some of us in some situations, He is. For others, such spending would be an unloving decision. Every decision must be guided by the question: Is this an expression of biblically sincere love, as described in the Scripture passages we've just studied?

When in doubt, sincere love errs on the side of generosity. And when we "lose" something for the sake of love, the Lord has a way of replacing our loss with something even greater (see Mark 10:28–30).

Two thousand years ago, a person was considered prosperous and able to help others if he or she owned a second coat or had a second loaf of bread in the pantry (Luke 3:11). The standard for determining "ability" may have changed since then, but the Lord's command to express sincere love by living modestly and sharing our abundance still applies today. Those who sincerely love the children of God will temper their consumption in order to give as much as possible from their time, money and other resources to help persecuted and suffering fellow believers.

We need to grow in knowledge and discernment about how to manage our abundance in view of the global needs of the body of Christ and the poor in general. I admit that for many years I did not contribute to the needs of persecuted Christians. At the time, I lived in half-ignorance, half-denial. I was preoccupied and comfortable with my life and the treasure of this world that makes a man lukewarm toward the kingdom of God and His children. By the Lord's grace I have since repented and the Lord is fanning into flames my otherwise shamefully lukewarm heart. As a result, I'm learning to live modestly and to temper my consumption so I can contribute more to my brothers and sisters in tribulation—that my love might be sincere: pure and without hypocrisy.

———— ⁓ ————

FOR THOUGHT AND DISCUSSION

Try applying the sincerity test to a spending decision you're facing. Which of your possible choices involves love that is . . .

- *Open and honest, rather than hiding?*
- *Pure and true, rather than polluted?*

Journaling space provided at the end of this book.

REAL LIFE IN CHINA

Whitewashing the Tomb

Have you heard? It seems that the Chinese government—that is, the Chinese Communist Party—has eased off on persecuting Christians in recent years. We now hear about the new policy allowing any Protestant church to worship openly; churches need only register with the Three-Self Patriotic Movement[17] (TSPM). And parallel provisions have been made for Catholics, Orthodox and other major faiths. We even see Bibles being freely carried, read and sold in Party-sanctioned churches. What wonderful developments! Who ever thought they'd see Christian freedom in communist China?

But don't believe everything you hear. All is not as it seems. Chinese communism is still threatened by Christianity; it still resists devotion to anyone or anything but the Party, especially all-out, biblical devotion to Jesus. The government is still cruel and militant. They're just getting sneakier about how to persecute Christians.

World opinion is important to China. Given today's technology and careful international scrutiny, the Chinese government can't violate human rights as blatantly as they once did. So they've switched tactics. They're trying to make the power of Christianity work *for* the Party by keeping Christianity under their collective thumb. Thus the invention of the Three-Self Patriotic Movement, which sometimes refers to itself as "the Chinese church." Some 57,000 local fellowships have complied with the government requirement to register with the TSPM. Why, then, do tens of millions of Christians still insist on gathering in illegal, unregistered "house churches" in every province and city throughout China?

The answer becomes clear when we understand the implications of TSPM membership. Let's start with the TSPM statement of faith. In this one statement are mandated the beliefs of all "legal" worshippers among China's estimated 150 million-plus Protestants. However, the Bible teaches that each individual believer in Jesus and each local church has both the right and the responsibility to examine the Scriptures carefully to make sure the teachings of any human authority are accurate.[18] The mere existence of a mandated creed or confession—let alone one devised by an officially atheist government—runs contrary to this biblical component of Christianity.

A closer examination of the TSPM statement of faith uncovers several subtle but significant theological "oversights." Most notably, it fails to state that Jesus' sacrificial death is the means by which He provided our salvation. In fact, actual Party-sanctioned TSPM teaching puts forth not the good news of Jesus' atoning death for our sin but rather a gospel based on social rules and the social benefits of Christianity.

Theology presents only one of many types of problems for a Bible-believing Christian trying to live his or her faith within the

TSPM. For registered churches, the Party decides how many people can be baptized per year and has the final say on who can preach and what can be preached. For example, preaching about the resurrection and the second coming of Jesus is forbidden; so is preaching against abortion.

Government officials, teachers, soldiers and police officers are not allowed to be Christians, no matter what their consciences might dictate. Even more tragic, under the TSPM no one younger than eighteen is allowed to be evangelized or to become a Christian. Imagine being a Christ-loving parent, waiting eighteen years, watching your child come up through the Party-run schools and being indoctrinated with Party brainwashing. Imagine spending your children's entire early lives ignoring the Lord's clear command to teach our children His Word (Deuteronomy 6:7; Ephesians 6:4). Imagine intentionally excluding the "little ones" from salvation. Jesus Himself said, "Let the little children come to me, and do not hinder them, for the kingdom of God belongs to such as these" (Mark 10:14).

Christian parents who abide by Communist Party regulations are consciously choosing to wait eighteen years to show their children the way to eternal life!

Well-intentioned visitors to China have observed the Three-Self churches and come away asking, "What's the big deal? Just register your church, and you can worship legally." And indeed some Three-Self churches—especially in certain regions where the government is permissive or passive toward the true church—are successfully doing the work of the gospel. Praise the Lord for these opportunities!

But as you may begin to see, it's impossible to live according to true biblical Christianity within the strictures of the Three-Self churches where Party rules are enforced. And so while 57,000 local churches have registered with the TSPM, several times this number of "house churches" have refused.

And they pay a price. The Party has become more subtle but no less oppressive in most regions. Jesus followers who refuse to toe the Party line are fired from their jobs, are evicted from their homes, or lose their electricity or water. The Party leans on employers, landlords and city officials to partner with them in oppressing uncooperative Christians. Also, congregations are evicted from their places of worship or have their buildings sealed or demolished; some of these congregations continue to worship outdoors, year round, through wind, rain and snow.

Although the Chinese government has recently shifted toward these "softer" tactics, it has by no means left behind its old habits—groundless arrests and detainments, imprisonment (often for several years in horrid labor camps), beatings, torture, rape and murder. In fact the number of reported instances of Christian persecution in China has increased every year for the last several years. Reliable sources indicate that these *reported* cases are only the tip of a huge persecution iceberg; Chinese brothers and sisters in Christ are persecuted by the thousands every year, yet the majority of these instances never come to light.

We've chosen one month—August 2013—from which we've summarized a sampling of reported persecution cases. This is an average month for Chinese Christians, and it turns up the following:

Saturday, August 3, Henan Province—Several tons of construction debris—rock and dirt—were dumped against the entrance to the two-month-old building of Sunzhuang Christian Church during the early morning hours. The church is even registered with the TSPM and has a building permit. But they've endured constant harassment, including an eviction notice, a demolition notice, loss of power and water, and one other instance when the entrance was sealed with tons of debris.

Sunday, August 4, Xinjiang Autonomous Region—The morning worship of Muen Church was interrupted when more than twenty police officers broke in, seized Bibles and other printed material from the several dozen believers and detained Pastor Tan Wen for fifteen days. This action was in retaliation for Pastor Tan's exercising his legal rights—filing an application and a lawsuit to protect the church's rights and property—after a previous church raid, detention and fine in June.

Wednesday, August 7, Hebei Province—An underground (unregistered) Catholic priest, Rev. Song Wanjun, was detained by ten law enforcement officials in the early morning hours. If he's treated like other Catholic priests in this province, he may be sentenced to several years' imprisonment and could be held indefinitely or killed. Two priests from this province—one currently eighty-two, the other ninety-two—were arrested in 1997 and 2001, respectively. Nothing is known about the whereabouts or even the survival of either man.

Sunday, August 11, Beijing—The Shouwang Church of Beijing has been meeting outdoors every Sunday for more than two years, since their every attempt to rent or buy indoor facilities has met with government intervention. Every Sunday dozens of Christians are arrested and detained; the pastor and elders have been placed under house arrest. On August 11, at least thirty-eight believers were arrested, and two-thirds of them were detained for several hours. One woman was seized by the throat and hair; in the past, church members have received severe beatings. Constant abusive questioning and threats are a routine part of the detainees' treatment. The Christians repeatedly respond with calm forgiveness and prayers on behalf of their oppressors, waiting in faith for "a nation full of love and righteousness."

Tuesday, August 13, Shanxi Province—Li Shuangping, the leader of Linfen house church, was ambushed and abducted at night from his car by four agents of local government. He was forced into another car, bound, blindfolded and beaten by three of the men while the other drove. One man issued violent, specific death threats against Li and his family, including his children—expressly because he's a house church leader. Li was eventually thrown out into a corn field and left to fend for himself.

Wednesday-Thursday, August 21-22, Shandong Province—On Wednesday, several police officers broke into the building used by Jiazhou Bay Christian Church and held the pastor's wife and several church members for several hours, threatening them and seizing their cell phones. The next day officials of the TSPM served an eviction notice, the latest in an ongoing campaign of intimidation and harassment. After being forced out of their previous building, church members contributed their own money and labor to make this run-down, Christian-owned hall habitable.

Posted August 22, incident date uncertain, Guizhong Province—A group of workers from the Religious Affairs Bureau, accompanied by local police, interrupted a house church meeting of more than twenty people. They detained the preacher and several church members, demanding that the church register with the TSPM. The Christians persistently refused and were left alone after several hours of "talking" (given threats and harassment).

Thursday, August 29, Henan Province—This day began the appeal hearing for seven Christians caught up in an April 2012 home church raid involving more than two hundred police and government officials. The seven were convicted in April 2013 of so-called "cult crimes," each sentenced to anywhere from three to seven and a half years in prison. In Thursday's appeal hearing, the defense lawyers spent the day confronting the chief judge and the judicial council with several instances of procedural improprieties that they, the judges, had perpetrated already. By the end of the day, the embarrassed chief judge announced a delay—the latest of many—and we have yet to learn when the appeal hearing will continue.

Saturday, August 31, Xinjiang Autonomous Region—Four Christians—a man and three women—were arrested for organizing a Sunday school for about forty middle and elementary school children and their parents. Their families were in immediate danger of being arrested, and the children of the four were interrogated. The four were held for fifteen days and fined.

Posted September 9, incident dates uncertain, Inner Mongolia Autonomous Region—Some time in August six Christians were arrested, held for fifteen days and fined. The crime? They continued to meet as a house church after being banned by the local Religious Affairs Bureau (RAB). The six were part of an unregistered fellowship that had split off from a TSPM church. They affirmed, with the Bible, that the church is led by the Lord; the official TSPM church position is that the church's leader is the Communist Party. The RAB also ransacked the group's building and beat several believers.

We've omitted several August reports because of space limitations. These stories represent a small fraction of the millions of Christians affected by government persecution—including huge numbers languishing out of sight in prisons, labor camps and detention facilities. Note that these ten incidents happened in eight Chinese provinces and municipalities, scattered from west to east, north to south, throughout this massive nation.

Don't believe the lie. China is still a dangerous place for Christians, and Christians are still suffering under oppression and persecution because they love Jesus. Speak up for them. And pray for them as if they were your own family. (They are.)

CHAPTER 10

Straining Gnats, Swallowing Camels

I've tried to make a biblical case for the following thesis: How much we help the least of the saints, according to our ability, is a litmus test that indicates how much we love them—which in turn reflects how much we love the Lord. It's up to you to study the Scriptures and decide whether this is true.

While on your journey, you may need to examine your doctrine on giving and ask whether it's supported by Scripture. Many American Christians today believe our financial obligation to the Lord and the body of Christ is a tithe (10 percent) of our income to our local church. After that, according to this school of thinking, we may give a little more but are free in God's eyes to spend the other 90 percent any way we wish.

But tithing is not authorized in the New Testament. A more detailed consideration of tithing in presented in my book *Prodigal's Progress: From Loving Money to Loving God*. In short, the New Testament is filled with early church teaching and examples of giving; however, Christian giving is never associated with a percentage. Nowhere in the New Testament does the Lord say that Christians should give 10 percent of their income. Nor are there any examples or inferences in Scripture to lead us to believe the early Christian church might have taught or practiced tithing.

The command to tithe originated in the Old Testament Mosaic law. At that time the Lord commanded His people to give an offering of two tithes (a total of 20 percent) every year and a third tithe (for a total of 30 percent) every third year.[19] In Acts 15:5–29, the Lord released us from tithing when the apostles said we need not observe the law of Moses except "to abstain from food sacrificed to idols, from blood, from the meat of strangled animals and from sexual immorality" (15:29).

Some people say that Jesus condoned tithing for Christians in Luke 11:42:

> Woe to you Pharisees, because you give God a tenth of your mint, rue and all other kinds of garden herbs, but you neglect justice and the love of God. You should have practiced the latter without leaving the former undone.

Consider also the parallel passage (Matthew 23:23–24), where Jesus continues, "You blind guides! You strain out a gnat but swallow a camel." Jesus wasn't teaching that Christians should tithe. Rather, He was rebuking the Jewish leaders, who were supposed to be living according to the Mosaic law. If Jesus had intended this passage to apply to Christians, we should be giving 20 percent every year and 30 percent every third year. However, the context and teaching in this passage is not about tithing but about the common human temptation and tendency to love money more than people. It's about our tendency to delude ourselves and deceive others by using religious traditions to mask our greed and self-indulgence.

Jesus' new command requires that we sacrificially share our abundance with our suffering brothers and sisters. This command cannot be reconciled with any teaching that limits our love-obligation to some degree below our ability. We cannot sincerely love one another while limiting our assistance to a percentage or any other standard that condones indulgence or hoarding while others suffer and die.

FOR THOUGHT AND DISCUSSION

Carefully reread John 13:34; 15:12–14; Romans 12:1; and 1 John 3:16–18. Keep in mind the original context and intended meaning when John and Paul wrote these words. Picture also the faces of our brothers and sisters whose stories you've been reading throughout this book. Then consider: How much of your income and other resources is the Lord calling you to contribute toward the needs of the persecuted in Christ? How much does the test of sincere love allow you to consume or keep?

Journaling space provided at the end of this book.

PART III

LOVE REVIVED

Let us consider how to stimulate one another to love and good deeds.

—Hebrews 10:24, NASB

CHAPTER 11

Heart Problems

In 1995, Ravi Zacharias summed up the American Christian response to persecution with the following statement: "Silence lurks where anguished voices should be heard." Ravi said this during the time of the first Sudanese holocaust, when American Christians were largely ignorant and indifferent toward the plight of our suffering brothers and sisters in Sudan.[20] During that same year, Michael Horowitz, fellow of the Hudson Institute and longtime friend of Dr. James Dobson, published an op-ed article about Christian persecution in the *Wall Street Journal*. He cited several examples of "growing and large-scale persecution" of Christians. He described Christians as the Jews of the twenty-first century and challenged American Christians to speak up on behalf of their persecuted brothers and sisters. Mr. Horowitz's article influenced Dr. Dobson to write the following in his "family news" letter from Focus on the Family:

> Most modern-day Christians in the affluent western nations seem utterly oblivious to the dire extremities to which Christians in Muslim and former Soviet nations are being pushed—with murder, rape, torture, slavery, imprisonment and confiscation of property growing at an exponential rate. . . .

Michael Horowitz's original column in the *Wall Street Journal* should have generated an outpouring of support from outraged believers around the country. Inexplicably, it brought little more than a yawn.

Dr. Dobson also included this quotation from Nina Shea's *In the Lion's Den*: "Millions of American Christians pray in their churches each week, oblivious to the fact that Christians in many parts of the world suffer brutal torture, arrest, imprisonment and even death—their homes and communities laid waste—for no other reason than that they are Christians."

Dr. Dobson's letter continued:

The shocking, untold story of our time is that more Christians have died this century simply for being Christians than in the first nineteen centuries after the birth of Christ. They have been persecuted before an unknowing, indifferent world and a largely silent Christian community.

Chuck Colson said, "When I see something like this, my heart aches because the believers here don't even know about it, don't care. We're not expressing moral outrage; we're not indignant of the indifference of the United States government towards this. And we ought to be marching in the streets because our brethren are being persecuted, imprisoned, beaten, sold into slavery, and butchered and we don't seem to care in this country."

In 1996, the National Association of Evangelicals (NAE) responded to Horowitz, Dobson and Colson's challenge by issuing a "Statement of Conscience." In this statement the NAE, which represents forty-five thousand congregations from over forty different denominations across the United States, confessed their "silence" and "culpability." They pledged "to end today's wrongful silence by Christians . . . in the face of mounting persecution of Christian believers" and "to do what is within our power to address persecution." Several large denominations, including the Southern Baptist Convention, the Episcopal Church, the Presbyterian Church USA, and the United Methodist Church, also passed denominational resolutions and issued letters of support for the Statement of Conscience.

After issuing their statement, the NAE was instrumental in founding the International Day of Prayer for the Persecuted Church and helped draw attention in Washington to religious persecution. The NAE also lobbied for the formation of the USCRIF (United States Commission on International Religious Freedom)—a federal interfaith commission that is responsible for reviewing international violations of religious freedom and making policy recommendations to the President, the Secretary of State and Congress.

CALLOUS CONSCIENCE

Not much has changed in the last two decades since the Statement of Conscience. On September 27, 2013, Kristen Powers, in an article in *The Daily Beast*, commented on today's US Christian indifference to persecution:

> One would think this horror might be consuming the pulpits and pews of American churches. Not so. The silence has been nearly deafening. . . . American Christians are quite able to organize around issues that concern them. Yet religious persecution appears not to have grabbed their attention, despite worldwide media coverage of the atrocities against Christians and other religious minorities in the Middle East.[21]

The USCRIF has since been marginalized and virtually suffocated within the bowels of the State Department's bureaucracy. The US government does not necessarily follow the USCIRF's recommendations. The current administration has failed to demonstrate interest in the welfare of persecuted Christians. For example, contrary to the USCRIF's recommendation, they decided not to include Nigeria or Pakistan on the commission's list of "Countries of Particular Concern," even though these countries are known to be among the worst perpetrators of heinous crimes and oppression against Christians. Our government has chosen to also ignore the renewed genocide of Christians and other non-Muslims in Sudan.

The US provides tens of billions of dollars in foreign aid to countries like Pakistan, Nigeria and Egypt, where Christians are severely persecuted. The US government could leverage its foreign aid program to advance religious freedom. But it doesn't.

The British human rights activist Wilfred Wong deftly described the root cause of our government's lack of support for persecuted Christians in the following statement: "If Christians themselves do not have a deep awareness and concern for these issues, then it is hardly surprising when their governments fail to reflect such awareness or concern."[22]

UNBROKEN SILENCE

To revisit one of the most egregious examples, Sudanese Christians, who endured twenty-two years of unimpeded extermination (from 1983 to 2005), now find themselves again in a "fiery trial" of "great persecution."[23] Sudanese President Omar al-Bashir, who we've seen was indicted by the International Criminal Court on three counts of genocide, has since embarked on another mission to kill hundreds of thousands of Christians and other non-Muslims who live in Sudan. In 2011 an emergency congressional hearing was convened by the House Foreign Affairs Committee to address this crisis. The State Department was conspicuously absent from the meeting. During the hearing, US Representative Frank Wolf (R-VA) said, "I think the church in the West really needs to do a better job of advocating for the persecuted church . . . the silence of the church in the West is absolutely incredible."

In 2010 a US congressman sent letters to two hundred Christian and media leaders asking them to speak out on behalf of persecuted Christians. No one responded to the letter. When each of the leaders was contacted in follow-up to the letter, only one replied by saying, "We'll pray for you."

During the week prior to the 2014 International Day of Prayer for the Persecuted Church, we reviewed the websites of the twenty largest denominations and 200 largest churches in America. On their home pages, nearly all of them advertised Veteran's Day or Thanksgiving-related "food for the hungry" programs. Only one of these websites mentioned the Day of Prayer for the Persecuted Church on their home page, and only eight of them listed it on their website's calendar of events or somewhere else on their websites.

This experience gave me the impression I wasn't the only American Christian guilty of ignoring the persecuted saints. Many of us are failing to understand Jesus' new command—its imperative nature and biblical application for the saints who are enduring the "fiery trial" of persecution.

Languishing Within Reach of Rescue

What do you see? Statistics or stories?

A quarter million Burmese refugees are languishing in India, Thailand and China, living in circumstances little better than those they fled. That's a statistic.

But a story begins like this: "Thirty-year-old Biathleng fled [Burma][24] for Delhi in June, with three children and a teenage wife." This is the first sentence of a *New York Times* report—our only snapshot of the day-to-day existence of these five individuals. Their five true stories are representative of the millions of individual, first-person stories that get lost in the statistics.

Let's consider the story of a young man, his teenage wife and their three little ones—a story that the five of them haven't simply read or heard about; they've lived every excruciating second.

This young Christian family left behind their homes and everything they knew. Why? Because Burma is now heavily militarized, ruled ruthlessly by the hostile Buddhist majority who have been persecuting Christians for more than five decades. Biathleng left behind discrimination and forced labor, false accusations and arbitrary detentions. He and his family fled summary executions and conscription of children off the streets for combat. They ran from rape and extortion and burning of homes and churches. Biathleng and his wife and children went in search of freedom to practice their faith, on a quest for authorities who might lend a just and sympathetic ear.

They went also in search of food, fleeing the unrelenting famine of their homeland. Burma's government offered no relief to the country's predominantly Christian minority and refused to allow humanitarian aid to the region where Biathleng's family lived.

Biathleng's family realized they weren't going to survive in their homeland, so they decided to cross into neighboring India. They gathered what they could carry and spent two days crossing the ten thousand-foot-high Arakan Yoma mountain range. That brought them to India's isolated Mizoram state, which is comprised of about 90 percent Christians.

Sounds ideal, doesn't it? Christian refugees among Christian hosts. A God-given opportunity for the family of Jesus to care for its own.

Not so. The reputation of the Lord and His church is soiled.

On the whole, the refugees are unwanted and unloved. Picture Biathleng—a father desperate to protect and provide for his young family—required to compete with Indian nationals for inadequate food, medical resources and jobs. More than once, Mizoram has sponsored movements to push the Christian refugees back across the border. The central Indian government refuses even to recognize the refugees' existence, let alone provide humanitarian treatment for those who have fled for their lives.

What about international relief? The United Nations High Council on Refugees (UNHCR) exists for the purpose of helping people like Biathleng find their way to survival resources and eventually to resettlement in a welcoming host country. Where is the UNHCR in India? Not in Mizoram state. In fact, the Indian government allows the relief organization to operate in only one city—Delhi, in the heart of the Indian subcontinent. In recent years more than ten thousand Burmese have traveled to Delhi in search of official recognition of their refugee status and the meager benefits that come with it.

In pursuit of their refugee cards, Biathleng and his family shared a vehicle going north from Mizoram state for three hundred miles, then managed train fare for the additional thousand miles west to Delhi.

Imagine bringing your tiny, impoverished family of five to Delhi, the fourth-most-populous city in the world, with more than twenty-two million people and a population density of thirty thousand per square mile. Imagine not knowing the language and searching its labyrinthine quarters for housing and other basics of survival. Biathleng found a home for his wife and three young children, together with four other "roommates." The nine of them still live in this single eight-by-twelve concrete room, part of a mazelike tenement building. Fifteen rooms—housing approximately one hundred men, women and children—share a single toilet. Drinkable water is scarce, so the family suffers chronic illnesses—jaundice, diarrhea and dysentery—and rarely leaves their tiny home. When they're able, they attend Sunday worship meetings and their oldest boy attends a small nongovernment school where he learns English and Hindi—languages essential for survival in Delhi. Otherwise they huddle in their concrete box day and night, hour after long hour; they cannot tolerate the city's pollution except when absolutely necessary, and someone must protect their few possessions from theft.

At the time of Biathleng's story, he was waiting for an appointment for his UNHCR refugee card. Because of limited access to the UNHCR and the organization's inefficiency, Biathleng can expect the process from beginning to end to require twelve to eighteen months. Some cases take years, and some people literally die waiting. Even if Biathleng and his family survive the wait, rejection is a real possibility. In the years that the UNHCR has been operating in Delhi, only a few thousand Burmese refugees have been approved, and only a few hundred new approvals are processed each year—not nearly enough to keep up with the thousands of new refugees arriving annually in Delhi.

The benefits of approval? Well, they don't include up-front financial support; India phased that out in 2011. The refugee card is not a work permit; that requires a separate application. The credentials don't protect their owners from rampant resentment and discrimination by their Indian neighbors. Legal protection? Police pay little heed when detainees produce their refugee cards.

So what do people wait a year or more to acquire? A limited medical reimbursement is available, payable several months *after* the medical expense is incurred. And some qualified refugees find third-country placement, mainly in Canada, the US, Australia and Europe.

Meanwhile the refugees pine away like prisoners, by the thousands, in the dust, heat, smog and cultural isolation of Delhi.

Religious and ethnic discrimination and abuse affect all the refugees. They arrive unable to speak Hindi or English, with no clear avenues for learning. When they're able to find work, they're underpaid, if paid at all. The government has set the poverty line at the equivalent of a little over two American dollars per day; many Burmese work twelve-hour days for close to half of that. Instantly recognizable as foreign, the Christians from Burma are subject to frequent harassment, assault and rape. Picture Biathleng, frantic to glean anything edible for his wife and children, taking the risk of scouring market sites at night for discarded or rotten vegetables, competing with locals and animals for the scraps.

Our brothers and sisters in Christ have been abused, starved and driven from their homeland in Burma. Our spiritual siblings have worked hard and traveled far in search of basic life necessities and the freedom to live for Jesus. And still they suffer.

Christians who have fled Burma to other countries are no better off. They flee east into Thailand, where, by recent figures, 140,000 Burmese refugees stagnate in isolated mountain camps. They flee north into China, where refugees have recently been deported by the thousands back to Burma—back into the thick of armed conflict and religious persecution—contrary to China's own law and violating international laws signed by China.

Think of all the unbelievers out there who have read the *New York Times* article about Biathleng's plight. They have good reason to scoff at Christianity, in light of the inactivity and apparent disinterest of Christ's global family. For the sake of our witness before the watching world, we *must* help. We must seek updated reporting about persecution in Burma, which is readily available online. We must pray fervently for our brothers and sisters in Burma and in equally horrendous circumstances as homeless refugees in neighboring countries. We must make our voices heard through the channels of power and influence, pressing Burma, India, Thailand and China to treat our family with dignity and care. And where secure avenues become available, we must share our wealth so that Biathleng and his little tribe might enjoy one or two healthy meals per day.

As it is, millions of Christian refugees suffer in the "havens" to which they've fled, hoping for our biblical hospitality. The world scoffs at the apparently uncaring Western church. The Lord weeps.

And for Biathleng, his wife, his three little children, this existence—every second, every minute, every hour, every day—is neither a story nor statistic. For them, it's life.[25]

CHAPTER 12

That the World May Believe

No one has ever seen God; but if we love one another, God lives in us and his love is made complete in us. (1 John 4:12)

Wouldn't it be wonderful if any honest unbeliever could observe the Christian community and inevitably come to the conclusion that Jesus is the only Savior, sent from God? Imagine if by our conduct these dear, lost people could see enough of God in us to cause them to trust us and listen to our message.

A dream, you say? Impossible? Well, it's Jesus' Plan A (and He didn't give us the option of any Plan B), and He made it our responsibility to bring it to reality. How? By obeying His command to love one another.

We opened this book with a look at Jesus' new command: to love one another in the same way Jesus has loved us (John 13:34). Now let me remind you of Jesus' next sentence: "By this all men will know that you are my disciples, if you love one another" (13:35). On the night before His impending crucifixion, Jesus was concerned about our witness before the watching world—and His plan for convincing the watchers was *agapē* love in all directions within the church.

Later that evening, Jesus prayed. He prayed for us. And in that prayer He revealed His plan, and the way that He longed to see it fulfilled:

> . . . that all of them [us, His followers] may be one, Father, just as you are in me and I am in you. May they also be in us *so that the world may believe* that you have sent me. I have given them the glory that you gave me, that they may be one as we are one: I in them and you in me. May they be brought to complete unity *to let the world know* that you sent me and have loved them even as you have loved me. (John 17:21–23)

The Lord's plan and design is that the world will see Him—His glory—through us as we model sacrificial brotherly love and unity in the body of Christ. Jesus said that our unity and *agapē* love for one another is our "glory"—given to us by the Lord (17:22). And the witness of this glory would cause the world to "believe" and "know" the saving truth about Him.

BOUND BY LOVE

> Jesus gives the world the right to judge whether you and I are born-again Christians on the basis of our observable love toward all Christians.
> —Francis Schaeffer

How often do we remember that our evangelistic success depends on *agapē* love flowing like blood throughout Christ's body? And how well do we understand that the body we must love is worldwide? Our sacrificial love is the bonding agent that unites the body of Christ and is therefore an essential prerequisite to successful evangelism.

> And over all these virtues put on love *[agapē]*, which binds them all together in perfect unity. (Colossians 3:14)

The early church modeled unity by their *agapē* love for one another, selling their possessions to provide daily food and other basic necessities for their poor brothers and sisters. They demonstrated pure and undefiled religion

(James 1:27), which powerfully validated Jesus as Lord and the authenticity of His disciples. This validation fueled rapid church growth in Jerusalem in spite of the high risk of persecution for those who decided to follow Jesus Christ. People were literally dying to follow Jesus—that's how strong was the early church's witness of love.

The apostle Paul's successful ministry is our biblical model for apologetics, evangelism, church planting and making disciples. It's no mere coincidence that Paul was also a passionate advocate and fundraiser for the persecuted saints. His ministry modeled the unity and *agapē* love that Jesus said would cause the world to know and believe that He was sent from heaven. Paul's tangible love for the suffering church was foundational to his evangelistic success.

In contrast, in American Christianity today we have impressive ministry plans and budgets for international justice, disaster relief, humanitarian aid and economic development for impoverished unsaved people in distant parts of the world. We appear to be doing incredibly great works for the severely impoverished and unsaved people around the globe in obedience to the Great Commission. These kinds of efforts are all good, all part of the Lord's purpose for His people.

But unlike Paul, we have developed an international reputation for not caring for our own—the Lord's suffering children. I spoke to an American church leader who attends conferences on persecution. He meets church leaders from persecuted countries, and they frequently ask him why American Christians are aloof and indifferent toward their suffering brothers and sisters.

How can watching non-Christians believe that Jesus is the Son of God, that we are His disciples, and that we love everyone, when it appears that we don't love the Lord's suffering children? How can the world believe that we love the Lord, whom we have not seen, if it appears we do not love our brothers whom we have seen (1 John 4:20)? As we saw in the preceding story about the forgotten Burmese refugees, as publicized by the *New York Times*, our hypocrisy obscures the beauty and excellence of Christ's body and hinders the world from knowing and believing that Jesus Christ is Lord.

Fifty years ago, Martin Luther King prophetically warned us, "If today's church does not recapture the sacrificial spirit of the early church, it will lose its authenticity, forfeit the loyalty of millions, and be dismissed as an irrelevant social club with no meaning for the twentieth century." The good news is that it's not too late. We can still demonstrate the sacrificial love that will cause our light to shine before people in such a way that they will glorify our Father who is in heaven (Matthew 5:16).

WILL WE PROVE FAITHFUL?

Earlier I referenced the op-ed that Michael Horowitz wrote at the time of the first Sudanese holocaust. In this article Mr. Horowitz added that the American Christian community's "moral authority will be gravely tarnished if it fails to exercise its growing political influence on behalf of people now risking everything to engage in the simple act of Christian worship and witness."[26] In other words, our witness will be worthless, and our moral message will be thrown out and trampled underfoot by men, if we do not turn from our hypocrisy and remember our brothers and sisters who endure prison and affliction.

Mr. Horowitz has been proven right. We've lost much of our moral authority and influence since his editorial was written twenty years ago. Are we willing to acknowledge that our sin of silence, while millions of our brothers and sisters have been murdered and inhumanely treated over the last twenty years, has contributed to the darkness that is overtaking America?

Our forefathers suffered and risked their lives so we could have religious freedom today. We're stewards of this liberty, and "it is required of stewards that they be found faithful" (1 Corinthians 4:2, ESV). If we fail to use our God-given, constitutional freedom of religion to obey the imperative of Jesus' new command, what hope do we have for the success of our evangelistic efforts? And what hope do we have that the Lord will hear our prayers and allow us to continue in this rapidly fading liberty?

You, my brothers and sisters, were called to be free. But do not use your freedom to indulge the flesh; rather, serve one another humbly in love. (Galatians 5:13, NIV-2011)

The context of this passage in Galatians is freedom from the law of Moses—a freedom belonging to every Christian. However, the principle also applies to economic and religious freedom, which is *not* the privilege of every Jesus follower, but currently entrusted to only the relative few. Our freedom and prosperity is a trust from the Lord that must be used for serving one another, locally and globally, in order to build up of the body of Christ.

Ravi Zacharias has succinctly summarized the consequences of our indifference towards our persecuted brothers: "The silence of the many on behalf of the some will only breed evil that ultimately destroys us all."[27] Zacharias is not suggesting that self-preservation is the primary motive in ministering to the persecuted saints; he's reminding and warning us, as Paul did: "Do not be deceived: God cannot be mocked. A man reaps what he sows" (Galatians 6:7).

In his book *The Future of Christians in the Middle East*, Dr. Habib Malik validates Zacharias's prediction. Dr. Malik is a Lebanese Christian with a Harvard doctorate in intellectual history, and he's a professor of history and cultural studies at Lebanese American University. He writes that Western indifference to the fate of Arab and other Middle Eastern Christians has contributed to their decline and peril. He also points out that our blindness has imperiled the West and that the defense of religious freedom for persecuted Christians in the Middle East is both a moral and strategic imperative.

The unsaved world is looking and longing for the perfect love that comes from above, which apart from Christ is nothing more than a hollow echo in the souls of men. What they see within the global body of Christ will not only influence their future, but perhaps ours as well. For the sake of their eternal salvation and for our continued enjoyment of liberty, we must express biblical love for God's persecuted children around the world.

REAL LIFE IN INDIA

Out-Castes for Christ[28]

Ten-year-old Namrata knows she's running for her life. The Hindus have already begun attacking homes in the village. They're literally out for blood—Christian blood.

Namrata scrambles and stumbles to keep up with her two sisters. Her eighteen-year-old sister, Trusita, is leading them through the night to the home where she works as a maid when she isn't in school. Maybe they'll be safe with the Das family—also a Christian household, but better off and less likely to be attacked than Namrata's family, a family of agricultural day laborers. A family of Dalits.

Dalits. The lowest of India's supposedly outlawed caste system. Dalits like Namrata are still treated as they're often called: "untouchable."

The Christians in Namrata's village have heard rumors of a wave of violence overtaking Orissa state in recent days. Three days prior, a well-known Hindu leader was assassinated. A Marxist group has taken responsibility for the killing, but this inconvenient fact isn't preventing Hindus from stirring up Orissa's Hindu majority, convincing them that Christians were behind the assassination and are trying to take over the country.

In a sense, the Hindus' fears aren't totally unfounded. Faith in Jesus Christ has been gaining a strong foothold in Orissa, India's poorest state. Orissa once reported only 2 percent Christian population. But since people have started coming to Christ by the thousands—especially among the Dalits and minority tribal peoples—even the Hindu nationalists have acknowledged that Orissa's Christian population has reached more than one in four. They're fearful of what would happen to India's Hindu purity and domination if Christians belonging to the lower castes were ever to exercise their full voting power. Intimidation and physical assualts are the Hindus' only hope for forcing these masses to return to Hinduism.

So when Namrata's parents received warning earlier this evening that the Hindus had begun attacking Christians and burning homes here in their village, they were ready to take action. After sending their children off to the Das household, they fled to the nearby forest to join other Christians to wait out the attack.

The three girls arrive at the Das home safely and are welcomed by the family. But soon their fears come true; they hear angry shouts approaching, then pounding on the door. Even this home won't escape the murdering marauders. The host family, along with Namrata and her sisters, hurry to hide in a small bathroom. The pounding on the door becomes more insistent, until they hear the door broken in and angry men entering, violating the sanctity of the home. Loud profanities. Smashing furniture, shattering crockery. Every crash, every shout makes Namrata jump.

Each time a new wave of cold washes over her from head to toe. *Make it stop!* she wants to scream.

Then . . . *smoke!* The house is being set on fire!

Namrata wants to run. It's so hard to hold still. But she knows escape is not yet possible. If anyone gives away their hiding place . . .

She has heard the stories, and throughout each long, terrifying minute her racing mind with its vivid imagination can't help replaying each horror in graphic detail. Stories of rape, torture, brutal murder. Stories of people doused with kerosene and burned alive.

The smoke seeping into the bathroom adds to her growing dread. Unthinkably horrific, to burn alive. Will it happen to her tonight? What else might the maddened invaders do to her if they find her?

In the darkness Namrata and her sisters cling to one another.

And Namrata clings to Jesus. Only He can bring them through this safely.

Dear Jesus, she prays, *please don't let the men find us. Please protect us from the fire.* She trembles in terror.

The noises gradually give way to silence. The cowering believers wait to be sure the attackers have actually gone. Slowly they open the bathroom door. Smoke billows in; they hear the crackling of flames, but no evidence of the attackers.

They stealthily emerge to a scene of roiling devastation. Flames lap and flicker here and there. Across the floors are strewn all the household's possessions, mostly in unrecoverable pieces.

They venture to the broken front door and open it a smallest fraction. In the distance they hear angry shouts, frightened screams, crashes and crackling flames. But the attackers have moved on; they're unlikely to come back.

While the others timidly make their way outside, ever watchful for danger, Namrata finds herself strangely fascinated by the ruin that surrounds her. She surveys the scene. Every dish lies in broken bits. Here a smoldering bed, there a pile of burning books. She walks past a dresser that is surprisingly intact.

Deafening blast! Instant inferno. Her body is thrust across the room, crashing against the opposite wall. All goes dark . . .

Namrata comes back to consciousness days later in a hospital eighty miles from her home. Her whole body hurts—especially her face. And what is all this white goo on her face? She touches it and starts to smile. But it hurts to smile. Why?

Her mother—overjoyed to see her daughter awake—explains. The attackers, before they left the house, planted a bomb in the dresser. It detonated just as Namrata was standing next to it. The explosion severely burned her face and left shrapnel wounds on her face, hands and back—over 40 percent of her body.

The day after the attack, her parents returned from the forest. When they first saw the Das home in charred ruins, they feared all had died in the flames. What joy to find that all were alive! Only to turn back to anxiety when they discovered the still-unconscious Namrata. They anxiously tended her on the long journey down from the mountains to the hospital at the coastal city of Brahmapur.

Namrata doesn't leave the hospital until mid-October, a month and a half later. Her recovery is long and her face will be disfigured the rest of her life. What thoughts and emotions does she grapple with during the long months of her healing? Trauma and fear. Embarrassment and shame at the permanent marring of her once-pretty face. Anxiety about her health and her future.

And anger. Who wouldn't wrestle with anger—even hatred—toward those who attempted to kill her entire family, who took away everything they owned, who damaged her body so horribly, whose continued threats still prevent them from returning to live among their friends and family?

The humble Dalit family spends a short time in an Orissa refugee camp before being relocated with the help of a Christian relief organization to the huge city of Bangalore, eight hundred miles away from their mountain village. Will they ever return? Or are they destined to live as wanderers, robbed of stability and security?

Perhaps Namrata strives mightily with these and other questions and emotions—a battle no ten-year-old should have to face. But in the end she rises the victor, for the autumn months prove to be a period of both physical and emotional healing. By the time she speaks with a news agency in December, she has achieved a settled peace that few mature adults reach, even after several decades of life experience.

Heed the words of a child: "We forgive the Hindu radicals who attacked us, who burned our homes." Namrata's attitude is nothing short of a miraculous demonstration of the Lord's Holy Spirit living inside her. She's grateful to be alive, trusting herself to the Lord's care. Her deepest desire is that her attackers might discover the amazing love of Jesus, come to salvation and spend eternity worshipping in heaven beside her.

Namrata loves Jesus. And Namrata loves her enemies. If she could, she would take them by the hand and lead them to Him.

In more than a dozen of India's twenty-eight states, violent persecution of Christians has been on the rise over the last many years. Christians by the hundreds are being murdered for their love of Jesus. Thousands more are beaten, tortured, raped and falsely arrested. Thousands of homes and churches have been burned.

The perpetrators are almost always Hindus. The police usually turn a blind eye to these activities, and sometimes it's even the "law enforcement" authorities themselves who step in as the brutal aggressors.

More than fifty thousand Orissa Christians fled their homes during the months of death and fear in which Namrata was caught up. Many lived for years in the forest or under tarps in refugee camps. Several years after the violence, many thousands remain homeless.

Those are large, impressive numbers. Now look past the numbers to the mass of personal pain and loss they represent. The cumulative grief, the collective sorrow. The terror and agony of those attacked, the suffering of those bereaved. The persistent confusion and uncertainty for those who have lost everything. The years of toil to regain some semblance of a normal life.

Meanwhile, Indian Christians like Namrata wish nothing but good toward their nation and their persecutors.

Namrata's face and body will never be the same. But while the outer Namrata might be wasting away, the inner Namrata is glowing brighter and brighter day by day.

"They were out of their minds," she explains, believing the best about her attackers. "They do not know the love of Jesus. For this reason, I now want to study so that when I am older I can tell everyone how much Jesus loves us." You see, Namrata has a plan for her life—a plan she believes comes from her Lord: She wants to spend the rest of her days sharing God's message. "This is my future."

Jesus is her inspiration. Pain is her strength. Love is her theme.

The future won't be easy for Namrata or her family. The lowly Dalit family possesses virtually nothing in material terms. But they all maintain joyous hope because of the eternal spiritual wealth they possess in Jesus Christ—a wealth they gladly share.

"The world has seen my face destroyed by the fire," Namrata says, referring to the picture of her scarred visage that has been posted across the Internet. "Now it must come to know my smile full of love and peace."

Beauty. Submission. Obedience. Forgiveness. Relentless love. These are the qualities that grow and blossom within a girl with the maturity to match her appearance—that of a wizened older woman. It's fitting that Namrata's family name, "Nayak," means "hero." Let us allow Namrata's example to inspire us to follow in her tiny bare footsteps.[29]

CHAPTER 13

Spiritual CPR

> When I heard these things, I sat down and wept. For some days I mourned and fasted and prayed before the God of heaven. (Nehemiah 1:4)

We know we should feel sad for the horrible things happening in other lands to our family in Christ. And sometimes, some of us do. But many of us don't.

The fact is that we can't manufacture genuine emotions on command. Genuine emotions arise from a heart of compassion that reflects God's burden for His people. We cultivate compassion when we gain an honest grasp of reality and engage it with a pure and open heart. If we don't experience sadness when we hear about our suffering spiritual siblings, it could be because we either don't have an intellectual understanding of their suffering or we're not allowing our hearts to become vulnerable enough to identify with them.

The first problem—failure to understand with our intellect—can be remedied simply by further exposure: Seek out reliable news of persecution, and be willing to listen to the painful details. But the second problem is more difficult to fix. Hardened hearts can't be penetrated by mere facts alone. In order to identify with our brothers and sisters at a heartfelt level, we must begin with prayer. We must be honest with the Lord about our lack of empathy or unwillingness to be involved, and He will help us to grow past it.

In this attitude of submissive prayer, we can choose to engage our hearts and exercise our God-given imaginations to identify more closely with the persecuted. We can picture their faces and imagine the ways they're just like us. We can put ourselves in their place, imagining what they must feel and fear. We need to humble ourselves, to recognize that we could just as easily have been born in their country and their circumstances; we've done nothing to deserve our material blessings and our freedoms. And generally speaking, they've done nothing to deserve their impoverishment and pain. The Lord distributes advantage and agony as He sees fit, and we who are entrusted with liberty and earthly abundance bear a weight of accountability for the distribution of our many benefits.

By the cooperation between our conscious choices and the Lord's enabling transformation, we learn to "rejoice with those who rejoice" and "weep with those who weep" (Romans 12:15, NASB). We will then exult in things that please the Lord and grieve for things that sadden Him—particularly for His children, suffering for His name.

It was with a desire for such change that I went before the Lord on August 25, 2009, asking Him to reveal His heart to me. I believe that I heard the word "Orissa," as if whispered into my heart, in response to my prayer. I also believe that the Lord led me to read 2 Samuel 11 and Nehemiah 1–2. (We'll come back to those Scripture passages in a moment.)

I was perplexed when I heard the word "Orissa"—the name of a state in India that I had encountered only once before, a year earlier, when I had learned that scores of Christians were killed by Hindu mobs who demanded they convert or be killed. Three hundred churches and six thousand Christian homes were looted and burnt down, and 56,000 Christians were left homeless.

After hearing "Orissa" while in prayer, I did some research and learned that more than ten thousand Christians were still—one year after the attacks, homeless, living in the jungle, while nearly ten thousand more were living in conditions only slightly better—under tarps in squalid refugee camps. They dared not return to their homes, where Hindus were still abducting and threatening to kill Christians who refused to renounce their faith in Jesus Christ.

I'm ashamed to admit I was not appropriately disturbed by what I learned. Twenty thousand or more of my Christian brothers and sisters in Orissa had been suffering and barely subsisting in the jungle and in refugee camps throughout the preceding year, and I was not genuinely troubled. But the softening of our hearts can take time, and the Lord is patient with us when we persist obediently toward His purposes in our lives. The Lord used the examples of two amazing men—Uriah and Nehemiah—to help me understand how godly men and women ought to respond in solidarity with our suffering brothers and sisters.

BAND OF BROTHERS

When we read the story of King David's sin with Bathsheba (2 Samuel 11), we naturally tend to focus on David. But let's review the story again, this time with careful attention to a different character—Bathsheba's husband, Uriah.

David saw Bathsheba bathing on her rooftop and sent for her, though she was married to one of his soldiers. They slept together and Bathsheba became pregnant. In a scheme to cover up his sin, David sent word to his general, Joab, to send Uriah back to Jerusalem with an update on the war. While Uriah was in Jerusalem he would certainly sleep with his wife—or so David thought—and her pregnancy would be attributed to him, not to David.

One problem: David did not take into account Uriah's love and loyalty to the Lord and his brothers.

David said to Uriah, "Go down to your house and wash your feet." So Uriah left the palace, and a gift from the king was sent after him. But

Uriah slept at the entrance to the palace with all his master's servants and did not go down to his house.

When David was told, "Uriah did not go home," he asked him, "Haven't you just come from a distance? Why didn't you go home?"

Uriah said to David, "The ark and Israel and Judah are staying in tents, and my master Joab and my lord's men are camped in the open fields. How could I go to my house to eat and drink and lie with my wife? As surely as you live, I will not do such a thing!"

Then David said to him, "Stay here one more day, and tomorrow I will send you back." So Uriah remained in Jerusalem that day and the next. At David's invitation, he ate and drank with him, and David made him drunk. But in the evening Uriah went out to sleep on his mat among his master's servants; he did not go home. (2 Samuel 11:8–13)

Since Uriah proved unwittingly uncooperative with David's cover-up, David finally sent Uriah into a certain-death situation on the battlefront, where Uriah was killed.

David is, of course, the more central character here. But the Lord directed me to this passage to show me the heart of Uriah. Here was a man who identified so closely with his embattled, imperiled brothers that he refused the simple luxuries of home when he had access to them. He could have gone home to his wife, but in solidarity with his brothers, he bunked in the servants' quarters, located at the palace entrance. Even the king's enticement couldn't persuade him to forget the glory of God and the well-being of his fellow soldiers.

At first glance, Uriah's situation might not seem very similar to ours. But make no mistake: Every believer in Jesus Christ is engaged in ongoing warfare. The genesis of the war and much of the conflict lie in the unseen spiritual realm. But the battle of the ages frequently spills out into the physical world, and those who suffer for refusing to deny Jesus are among the bravest of the Lord's warriors.

We need to closely identify with these heroes on the battlefield. In order to cultivate solidarity with our suffering brothers and sisters, we must consciously recognize the true unity of all believers with each other in one body. In this awareness, we must purpose to engage in the spiritual war effort as godly fellow soldiers. This is the rightful duty of every true Christian. As we become more consistently engaged in the battle, we will naturally become even more mindful of our oneness with the persecuted and grow to love them like brothers in battle. Just as Uriah loved his fellow combatants.

It's this love and compassion that moves us to "remember the prisoners, as though in prison with them, and those who are ill-treated, since you yourselves also are in the body" (Hebrews 13:3, NASB). When we cultivate hearts like Uriah's, we hear of the Orissa crisis and think, *God's people are sheltering under tarps and trees, eating whatever they can find in the jungle. How can I go about my "normal life" as though they weren't there, suffering? I have to help.*

A HEART FOR GOD = A HEART FOR HIS PEOPLE

The other passage to which I sensed the Lord directing me was about another man with a heart after the Lord and a love for His people. Nehemiah was one of the Jewish exiles scattered throughout the Persian Empire after the Lord destroyed Israel as a kingdom. The Lord blessed Nehemiah's faithfulness and raised him to a position of influence and favor in the Persian emperor's court: He was the royal cupbearer. One day he welcomed some visitors who had just traveled from the homeland he had probably never seen.

> I questioned them about the Jewish remnant that survived the exile, and also about Jerusalem. They said to me, "Those who survived the exile and are back in the province are in great trouble and disgrace. The wall of Jerusalem is broken down, and its gates have been burned with fire."
>
> When I heard these things, I sat down and wept. For some days I mourned and fasted and prayed before the God of heaven. Then I

said: "O LORD, God of heaven . . . let your ear be attentive and your eyes open to hear the prayer your servant is praying before you day and night for your servants. . . . They are your servants and your people, whom you redeemed by your great strength and your mighty hand. O Lord, let your ear be attentive to the prayer of this your servant and to the prayer of your servants who delight in revering your name. Give your servant success today by granting him favor in the presence of this man." (Nehemiah 1:2–6,10–11)

This prayer was six months in the making—from the fall of the year, when Nehemiah received the distressing news, to one day the next spring— the day he would petition the king for permission to go and help his people.

I was serving the king his wine. I had never before appeared sad in his presence. So the king asked me, "Why are you looking so sad? You don't look sick to me. You must be deeply troubled."

Then I was terrified, but I replied, "Long live the king! How can I not be sad?" (Nehemiah 2:1–3, NLT)

Nehemiah went on to explain his grief. The Lord had planted such a love for Nehemiah in the king's heart that the king gladly granted Nehemiah's every request, including letters of passage and even a mounted military unit for protection.

As I read Nehemiah's story, the Lord was drawing my attention to the example of a broken-hearted, godly man. Much as I had inquired of my Christian siblings in Orissa, Nehemiah had inquired about the welfare of his countrymen back in Judah. The circumstances for God's people in devastated Jerusalem were similar to the Christians' plight in twenty-first-century Orissa. In both situations His people were "in great trouble" or "great distress" (NASB), having been driven from their burning homes.

The greatest *dis*similarity in this comparison was between Nehemiah's response and mine. I was beginning to feel compassion—the Holy Spirit was starting to soften my heart—but Nehemiah spontaneously slumped and wept. Such was the relationship he had already cultivated with the Lord, and such was his affinity with God's people. His first several days of mourning, fasting and prayer stretched into months; his sorrow was so obvious half a year later that the leader of the then world power took notice.

Centuries before Christ's advent, Nehemiah modeled what it means to "bear one another's burdens, and thereby fulfill the law of Christ" (Galatians 6:2, NASB). He embodied the principle that when "one member suffers, all the members suffer with it" (1 Corinthians 12:26, NASB). Nehemiah's faith and love proved to be genuine because they moved him to action and sacrifice. He risked the emperor's disfavor—a prospect never to be taken lightly!—in order to come to his people's aid. His response to his brothers' crisis was "Send me."

As we seek and know the Lord, our affections will come into line with His. If we remain mindful of our solidarity with God's people, our emotions will more and more naturally become what they should be. Keep practicing faithful dependence on the Lord, and your love will grow. And the outflow will be a strengthening current of fervent love, prayer, action and sacrifice for our persecuted brothers and sisters.

As for the saints who are in the earth,
They are the majestic ones in whom is all my delight.
(Psalm 16:3, NASB)

FOR THOUGHT AND DISCUSSION

When you learn about the horrible suffering of your spiritual family, you may take Nehemiah's words as a question for yourself: "How can I not be sad?" Take a few minutes and conduct an honest heart check. Our emotions—our joy and our sadness—are often a reflection of what we treasure. We mourn for the loss of whatever genuinely matters to us. As we learn to delight in the Lord's "majestic ones" (see Psalm 16:3, above), we'll naturally cultivate a heart of compassion that grieves for their suffering.

What makes you weep?

Journaling space provided at the end of this book.

REAL LIFE IN NIGERIA

A Year in Memoriam

As I read reports on suffering and persecution, I find myself struggling inwardly, torn between two realities: my life of freedom and comfort and the lives of my suffering brothers and sisters. How can these two realms exist at the same time on the same globe? What exactly does the Lord intend by granting me such privilege when others suffer such grief and tribulation?

For me this is a difficult but spiritually healthy struggle. By identifying with my persecuted brothers and sisters, I begin to identify and fellowship with Jesus in a way that might be available only to the persecuted and to those who choose to carry their burdens. It also provides me with much-needed reminders: that this is not my home, and I'm an alien here; that my hope is in the Lord—I look forward to His return and the city "whose architect and builder is God" (Hebrews 11:9–10). (In a very small but important way, it also helps prepare me for the surreal anti-Christian sentiment and growing backlash against Christians in the US.)

Please join me in the struggle. Let's experience and remember together one year—2012—in the death and difficult life of Christians in Nigeria. Let's memorialize the dead and stand with the faithful living.

Background

Nigeria is home to nearly one-fourth of all sub-Saharan Africans. Its population is evenly divided between the Muslims, who are dominant in the North, and Christians, who form the majority in the South, with a belt across the middle equally mixed with both Christians and Muslims. Especially since 2009, Islamists have more and more boldly terrorized the northern and central states, sometimes killing Christian children, women and men by the hundreds.

Boko Haram—linked to al-Qaida and the Taliban—is the Islamic group responsible for most of the violence. They attack even fellow Muslims who don't practice the group's purist version of Islam. But Boko Haram is not alone; many bloody incidents involve average Muslims continuing a decades-long history of deadly persecution of Nigerian Christians.

January: *Warning and Warfare*

On the second day of the New Year, Nigerian Christians awake to a published warning to leave the North within the next three days or face death. Christians are still reeling from Christmas attacks on churches in six northern and central cities. More than fifty were killed; the bereaved have only just buried their dead.

Hundreds of thousands of Christians have already fled their homes in the North, though most are indigenous to the region and feel they have nowhere else to go.

Thursday, January 5, Gombe state—The three-day deadline passes; the terrorists make good on their threat. A gunman bursts into a service at Deeper Life Church, kills six, including the pastor's wife, and injures at least eight. *Mubi town, Amadawa state*—At least four Christians are killed by gunmen.

Friday, January 6, Mubi, Amadawa—Christians gather at a town hall to mourn and plan funerals for those killed the day before; the same gunmen enter and kill at least seventeen. *Yola, Amadawa*—Masked gunmen kill ten at the Apostolic Church. *Borno state*—A Christian couple is murdered.

Across the North, hundreds flee.

Sunday, January 8 (estimated date), Bauchi—Terrorists use guns and machetes to massacre three Christian farmers on their farms.

Friday, January 20, Kano—Coordinated attacks on eight government locations, including four police stations, kill more than two hundred, reportedly because of terrorist suspects held in custody in the city.

Sunday, January 22, Bauchi—A Catholic church and an Evangelical church are bombed without casualties. A security checkpoint is attacked, killing two soldiers, a policeman and eight civilians, including seven Christians.

February: *"Simply Because It's a Church"*

Four straight days of violence start the month in northeastern Adamawa state. Islamists attack three different Churches of the

Brethren on the first three days, and revisit the first one on February 4. Eight Christians and seven others are killed; three church buildings and numerous Christian homes are burned down. Christians fear attending services or even leaving their homes at night; some have had to close down their businesses. Fourteen of the denomination's pastors have been killed in Nigeria's violent Northeast, but the denomination president declares, "Hope is not lost. . . . A difficult situation cannot stop the Word of God."

A bombing of Christ Embassy church in northwestern Niger state on Sunday, February 19 injures five. On the following Sunday, Boko Haram claims responsibility for a suicide bombing in the Church of Christ in Jos, in central Plateau state; three Christians, including a toddler, are killed, and thirty-eight are injured. The Boko Haram spokesman says, "We attacked simply because it's a church and we can decide to attack any other church. We have just started."

March: *Words and Worse*

Captured Boko Haram leaders boast of their plan to "Islamize Nigeria" by taking down the current government, replacing it with Islamic law, and by attacking churches and any schools that don't "conform to our practice."

On Tuesday, March 6, Boko Haram attacks a Roman Catholic Church, a Church of the Brethren, a police station and a government building, killing at least two in Borno state. The following Sunday, a suicide car bomber targets a Catholic church in Jos, killing ten, including two boys, ages eight and sixteen.

April: *Sacrifices on the Altar*

Easter Sunday, April 8, holds unexpected terror for worshipers at All Nations Christian Assembly, Kaduna state. At least thirty-eight offer the greatest sacrifice; they fall victim to a suicide car bomber during service.

On Tuesday evening, April 24, a crowd of hundreds of Christians gather to watch soccer at a TV viewing center in Jos. A drive-by attacker throws an explosive device into the crowd, killing one.

And on April's last Sunday, gunmen on motorcycles throw explosives into a worship service at Bayero University, Kano state. They open fire on those fleeing the explosions, killing nineteen and wounding dozens, then riding away. Later the same day, in Borno state, gunmen enter the Church of Christ in Nigeria, killing the pastor and four others.

Nigerian Christians are urged to respond neither violently nor passively, but through "aggressive love," reaching out to help Muslim neighbors.

May: *No Greater Love*

On May 11, at the memorial service for the ten Catholics slain at the university, the bishop of Kano Diocese declares that persecution "should not weaken our resolve to remain faithful to Christ, but should make us strong."

In a sequence of terrorist attacks in fifteen Christian villages clustered in three regions of Plateau state, forty-four of our brothers and sisters lose their lives in horrific circumstances. Some are slashed and stabbed in their sleep with machetes and knives. Many children—including at least one infant killed with a machete—are among the dead. Dozens are injured and maimed.

More than a thousand have either had their homes destroyed or are afraid to return to their homes; they take refuge where they can, many in schools, without food or medical care.

Worshippers persist in church attendance. Their defiant spirit is evidenced by "joyous bursts of singing" amid "bouts of fiery preaching and concentrated prayer."

June: *Fire and Darkness*

Boko Haram resurfaces for their busiest month since January, carrying out six coordinated attacks on three consecutive Sundays.

Sunday, June 3—Twenty-one are killed and forty-five injured in a car bomb attack on Living Faith Church and nearby Harvest Field Church, Bauchi state. One survivor reports hearing cries of members in the midst of darkness as fire engulfed the church. Tragically, eight of the deaths and twenty of the wounded are due to bullets fired by security forces into crowds of Christians who gather after the bombing to mourn their loved ones and to protest the government's inadequate protection.

Sunday, June 10—A suicide car bomber targets the Christ Chosen Church of God in Jos, killing four and injuring more than forty. The same day, gunmen open fire on worshippers inside the Church of the Brethren in Nigeria, Borno state, killing two and injuring several others.

Sunday, June 17—Three suicide car bombers attack three churches in Kaduna state—the Evangelical Church Winning All, Christ the King Catholic Church and Shalom Church. The blasts kill a total of more than fifty, including women, children and an army

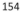

sergeant, and leave hundreds wounded—many so critically that the death toll is expected to rise.

July: *"I Enjoy Killing"*

On Saturday, July 7, Christians in twelve villages around Jos are terrorized when hundreds of armed attackers, some disguised in police uniforms, make their deadly way through the villages. Several hundred people have fled the violence and are homeless.

On that day, in the village of Maseh, some fifty members of the Church of Christ in Nigeria take refuge in their pastor's house, only to be trapped there and burned alive.

On Sunday afternoon, mourners on their way to a mass burial for Saturday's victims are attacked.

All told, the death toll for the weekend is more than one hundred, including two policemen and two legislators who had joined the funeral procession.

The following Tuesday, Pastor Ayo Oritsejafor, president of the Christian Association of Nigeria, testifies before a US House subcommittee, pleading with the US government to declare Boko Haram a terrorist organization. The group's leader, Abubakar Shekau, acknowledged individually as a terrorist by the US, has issued YouTube statements such as this: "I enjoy killing anyone that God commands me to kill—the way I enjoy killing chickens and rams."

August: *Death at Deeper Life*

On a Monday evening, August 6, worship is shattered when gunmen wielding Kalashnikov assault rifles surround Deeper Life

Bible Church, Kogi state, and open fire. Reports indicate as many as twenty-five are killed, including a pastor.

September: *The Four and the Forty-Eight*
Four are killed—including a woman and a child—and more than forty-eight injured on Sunday, September 23, when a suicide car bomber detonates near congregants emerging from the first service at St. John's Catholic Cathedral Church in Bauchi.

The Nigerian faithful bury their dead.

October: *Hope Amid Horror*
The month begins with nighttime raids on three colleges. Attackers search room to room, sorting Christians from Muslims, killing as many as forty-five Christians by shooting them or slashing their throats. This happens in Mubi, Adamawa state, where Christians have suffered some form of violent attack nearly every day for eleven months.

CBN-TV declares Nigeria "a Christian killing field." Yet in the midst of the horror, reason for hope arises.

Even as Christians are being targeted for death, they pray for their enemies. And the Lord answers. One Boko Haram member reads the good news of Jesus Christ and comes to faith in Him. He witnesses to other members and miraculously still lives. Others see the "goodness of the Christian religion" in the lives of Jesus' followers, and although they're not ready to place their faith in Christ, they warn Christians of impending attacks.

On the last Sunday of the month a suicide bomber disguised as a Christian attacks St. Rita's Catholic Church in Kaduna, killing at least fifteen and injuring about 150 others. Inside, as people express their love to Jesus, they discover the building falling down on them. The archbishop of Kaduna Diocese grieves that 90 percent of the victims are children, yet he calls Christian youths to abandon all thought of reprisal.

November: *Ten Minutes Later*
On Sunday, November 25, worshippers are five minutes into their service at St. Andrew Military Protestant Church, Kaduna state. A bus loaded with explosives drives into the side of the building and explodes. More people gather to help the injured when, ten minutes later, another suicide bomber arrives and detonates his cargo, killing more than the first explosion.

December: *Holy Night*
In Yobe and Borno states, gunmen raid the Church of Christ in Nations and the First Baptist Church after midnight Christmas Eve services, slaughtering at least a dozen worshippers, including a pastor. Several Christian families are attacked in their homes.

Year end brings the confirmable number of Nigerian Christian martyrs for 2012 to more than nine hundred.

2013–Present: *Still Fatal, Yet Faithful*
The martyrdom of the Nigerian saints continues. And so does their relentless faith.[30]

Lament

Mourn with families left fatherless or motherless,
for the children who will never again
see that parent's smile or feel their hug.

*Grieve with bereft mothers and fathers over the
murder of their children.
Heaven welcomes the young martyrs.
Sorrow for flocks who have lost their shepherds.*

*Share the burden of pain and restraint with
Christians who would seek vengeance.
Understand the fear and hatred with which
many struggle daily.
Pray for their purity and peace.*

*Learn faith, courage and perspective
from the Nigerian faithful.
Join in heartfelt appeal for the
salvation of the murderers.*

*Remember not only the dead,
but also the scarred and maimed,
the traumatized and the terrorized who live on.
Pray for their healing, both physically and spiritually.*

*"Don't be quiet.
Speak up to your government . . .
speak up to your church, support us."*[31]

CHAPTER 14

The Proof of Your Love

I speak on behalf of my brethren who lie in countless nameless graves. I speak on behalf of my brethren who now meet secretly in forests, basements, attics, and other such places.

The message I bring from the Underground Church is:

"Don't abandon us!"
"Don't forget us!"
"Don't write us off!"
"Give us the tools we need! We will pay the price for using them!"

This is the message I have been charged to deliver to the free Church. I speak for the Underground Church, the silenced Church, the "dumb" Church, which has no voice to speak.

—Richard Wurmbrand, *Tortured for Christ*

Throughout this book, in some words or other, we've heard the same message from Jesus, from John, from James and from Paul: *You say you love? Prove it!*

Show these men the proof of your love . . . so that the churches can see it. (2 Corinthians 8:24)

Our love for Jesus and our brothers and sisters in the body of Christ has to be more than a profession—it must produce *action*. Words alone are worse than weak; they're worthless. Nobel Peace Prize nominee Mama Maggie Gobran said the same: "When you love somebody—you live it."[32]

One high-priority means by which the Lord requires that we demonstrate our love is to minister to persecuted Christians. And you don't have to travel overseas. There's much you can do to help right in your home or church.

Nehemiah's example provides us with a four-part action plan. First, he took a proactive interest in the circumstances and relevant events affecting his people (1:2). Second, when Nehemiah heard the news about his brothers' circumstances, he "fasted and prayed before the God of heaven" (1:4). Third, Nehemiah advocated on behalf of his brothers and sisters (2:3–8). And fourth, he ministered practically to his people's physical needs—carrying out fundraising activities and donating from his own wealth (5:14–19; 7:70). Similarly, each of us is able in our own way to prove our love for the persecuted saints through these responses:

- Awareness
- Prayer
- Advocacy
- Relief and development

AWARENESS: OPEN YOUR MIND TO THE MUTE

The first way we can prove our love for the persecuted is simply by seeking to know about their circumstances. We demonstrate the proof of our love by taking an active interest in the issues and events that affect them.

Have you ever gone through a difficult trial and had someone else—maybe even a stranger—ask with genuine interest about how you're doing in that circumstance? Even if they couldn't do anything else to help, your spirits were lifted just by knowing that someone cared enough to inquire. You knew you weren't alone. In the same way, our pursuit of awareness about our suffering spiritual siblings is an important expression of love and a meaningful ministry to those who suffer.

Even more, awareness is a necessary prerequisite to any other measures we might take to help. We need to know about specific circumstances and needs before we can respond effectively with the other three categories of support—prayer, advocacy and assistance. For example, if we seek awareness of current events in Pakistan, we would learn that Pakistani lawmakers (at the time of this writing) are proposing legislation that would make it illegal to own a Bible in Pakistan. We would come to understand that for our two to three million Pakistani brothers and sisters, the passage of this law could be even more devastating than the current blasphemy law, which is frequently used to falsely accuse, attack and imprison Christians. We could then specifically pray that this law would not be passed. We could also pray that the Lord would also cause the blasphemy law to be repealed.

If we seek awareness of current events in Sudan, we would know that President al-Bashir has renewed his efforts to "cleanse" Sudan of all remaining Christians, just as Haman had hoped to annihilate the Jews in the biblical story of Esther. Out of this awareness would naturally emerge our further expressions of love—including our informed, fervent petitions to the Lord to save and change al-Bashir's heart and, if necessary, bring him to justice, as the Lord did to Haman in response to the prayers of Esther and her people.

The world does not share our passion and concern for God's children. Nor should we expect them to. As we've seen, we cannot count on the world and its media to provide us with current, complete and accurate information on Christian persecution.

We have to seek and use alternate sources for news—most of which are available through the Internet—in order to learn about the needs and circumstances of our persecuted family. Several organizations exist with connections to reliable, first-hand, in-country sources throughout the world—organizations committed to disseminating the disturbing truth in order to stir us to action and intervention. They're doing their part in order that we might do ours. Visit their websites, including our own *www.MuteNoMore.com*. Appendix B in this book includes a list of ministries that provide news, guidance for prayer, advocacy or relief for persecuted Christians. Sign up for their news feeds, follow them on social media, place links to these websites on yours, and take other action to gain information and to make information available to others. Persecution news should be made a priority in our homes and churches. It should receive prime placement on church websites, in bulletins and in other communications. Every church should designate one or more "ambassadors" responsible for providing regular news updates to their local church.

PRAYER: OPEN YOUR HEART FOR THE MUTE

The second activity that proves our love is prayer on behalf of the persecuted. When Nehemiah had received the sorrowful report about the Lord's people and their city, he "wept, mourned and fasted and prayed before the God of heaven" (Nehemiah 1:4). He persisted in expectant prayer for six months before the Lord's answer came.

I recall a time when I was feeling helpless and overwhelmed by the widescale nature and intensity of global persecution. I prayed and asked the Lord what I could possibly do to help my brothers and sisters. In my spirit I clearly heard the command, "Pray." So I began to pray for the safety of Christians in Indonesia and Nigeria. I later read that about the same time I was praying, three thousand pounds of explosives were found next to a church in Indonesia. The explosives had been placed next to a gas main at the side of the church, but a mechanical failure kept them from exploding. Praise the Lord! I also read that about this time a bomb was thrown into a Nigerian church during a service, but it failed to detonate.

I'm not suggesting my prayers were the sole reason these bombs did not explode. However, I do believe the Lord was teaching me that we can make an important difference for our brothers and sisters in danger, prison and affliction . . . simply by remembering them in our prayers. Why do so many of us fail to pray for the persecuted? For some, our silence before the Lord's throne might be rooted in ignorance and indifference. When I recognized this in myself, I began by confessing my indifference and made the conscious decision to begin regularly reading persecution news. This step alone caused my compassion and prayers to increase considerably.

Imagine how interested, prayerful and active you would be if your own biological family members were being unjustly punished or imprisoned in a foreign country. Picture your mother or father, your son or daughter, your brother or sister suffering at the hand of some oppressor overseas. How much would you pray for them? Would you ever stop praying? To what other lengths would you go on their behalf? This is how engaged we must be in fervent prayer and action on behalf of our persecuted brothers and sisters, "as though in prison with them" (Hebrews 13:3, NASB).

Among other things, our prayers for the saints in tribulation should include the following petitions:

- That through them, the Lord's Word and reputation will spread rapidly, and He will be glorified (2 Thessalonians 3:1)
- That those who oppose them might come to salvation in Christ
- That the Lord would grant them spiritual maturity, endurance, provision and protection
- That they will be mercifully delivered from perverse and evil men (2 Thessalonians 3:2)

You can find more guidance for your prayers in Appendix C of this book. As you pray, *watch!* Keep your eyes open for the Lord's answers. Watch for prisoners who are released, for governments that fall or change policy and for Christians who are allowed to return safely to their homes. And even when difficult circumstances don't change—or become worse—*listen!* Listen for the glowing testimonies of faith and love, honed and strengthened under unimaginable pressure and stress. Be humbled by these examples of Spirit-enabled fortitude, learn from them, and keep praying.

In the months leading up to this writing, the informed prayers of Christians around the world bolstered the faith of a twenty-seven-year-old Sudanese woman named Meriam Ibrahim. She and her mother had been abandoned by her Muslim father when she was young, and her mother raised her in the Christian faith. By God's grace, Meriam trusts and loves Jesus.

Meriam is married to Daniel Wani, who is a Christian and US citizen. Daniel is confined to a wheelchair with muscular dystrophy. Together, they have a two-year-old son, Martin, and a baby daughter, Maya. On May 15, 2014, Meriam was eight months pregnant with Maya when her faith was severely tested. She was arrested and convicted of adultery because of her unrecognized marriage to a Christian. She was also convicted of apostasy—for supposedly abandoning the Muslim faith of her long-gone father. Her so-called "adulterous" marriage earned her a sentence of one hundred lashes. Her "apostasy"—her all-out love for her Lord—drew a sentence of death by hanging. The lashes were postponed until she recovered from giving birth, and her execution until she weaned baby Maya. Meriam gave birth to Maya while in shackles and chains. Both of her children were kept in prison with her, even though they are Americans by virtue of their father's citizenship.

At one point, Sudanese Judge Mohammed Al-Khalifa gave Meriam the opportunity to abandon Jesus Christ and return to Islam. Our sister faced the gravest decision of her life: What would she love more—her life or her Lord? Was her commitment to Jesus strong enough that she could leave her children motherless and her wheelchair-bound husband a widower? Would she trade her remaining natural days on earth for an early entrance into eternal glory?

Meriam faced the man who seemingly held her physical destiny in his hands. With strength born of many prayers, she proclaimed her steadfast commitment to Him who had granted her eternal life. Heaven rejoiced, and God was glorified.

Thousands of Meriams and Daniels around the world are depending on and desperate for your prayers for strength and courage. If a little accountability, structure and guidance would help you pray effectively, then take advantage of the on-line prayer features available through various ministries' websites, newsletters and other avenues of communication. For example, our website's prayer wall *(www.MuteNoMore.com/prayer-wall)* invites you to start with a commitment as small as fifteen minutes per week. We also offer an e-mail and SMS text prayer guide and newsfeed. Several of the organizations listed in Appendix B also provide similar prayer guidance.

Imagine what will happen when more of us—tens of thousands, even millions of us!—begin praying regularly and fervently, equipped and guided by accurate information about current events around the world. What might happen when we, like Nehemiah, begin fasting and crying out together for, say, the North Korean children of God? What might the Lord, the Authority who governs all authorities, do in the hearts and circumstances of leaders like Kim Jong-un, the dictator in that country? When He's ready, the Creator can at once annihilate that corrupt government—or redirect a tyrant's heart and mind.

Imagine the Lord's perspective at this moment on our prayers for the persecuted—on the resounding silence on this topic emanating from so many of our prayer closets. Currently, He hears a whisper here, a mutter there from across the Western world. But what if the whispers multiplied and spread? What if the tiny trickle swelled to a stream, then a torrent? What if mediocre souls began to burn with desperate, confident fervor, and muttering gave way to shouts of vicarious pain, then victory?

ADVOCACY: OPEN YOUR MOUTH FOR THE MUTE

The proof of our love is also seen in our willingness to speak on behalf of our brothers and sisters whose voices cannot be heard. True love cannot remain silent while those we say we love are being tortured and killed for our common faith.

Open your mouth for the mute,
for the rights of all the unfortunate.
Open your mouth, judge righteously,
and defend the rights of the afflicted and needy.
(Proverbs 31:8-9, NASB)

Congressman Frank Wolf once gave a speech in which he quoted Chinese human rights lawyers, who said "that their lives improve, and those of their cohorts in prison or facing other pressures by the Chinese government, when the West speaks out for their plight and raises their cases by name."[33] In an interview with the *Christian Post*, Congressman Wolf was asked if it helps when people advocate for those being persecuted. He answered, "It always helps. Every dissident always told me that, when people advocate for them, it improves conditions. If you are a dissident in prison and people start sending letters to the government or even to the commandant of the camp, your life gets better. . . . Sometimes it helps them get out of prison, or they get a little more food. Always stand with them because it really makes a big difference."

According to Christian Solidarity Worldwide, "Lobbying to influence decision makers has in the past resulted in dramatic improvement for prisoners and victims of religious persecution. Torture has been stopped, access to doctors or lawyers has been granted, death sentences have been overturned and prisoners have been released. All governments, even the most repressive ones, dislike bad publicity because they depend on claiming legitimacy and authority. Exposing the illegal and inhumane acts of repressive regimes damages their trade, their tourism and their world standing."

While we're petitioning our Lord in prayer, we need also to petition our government, the United Nations and other world leaders to exert their substantial influence to change specific persecution situations. You'll recall Meriam Ibraham, our Sudanese sister in Christ, whose story you read earlier in this chapter. While she awaited her flogging and execution, news of Meriam's difficulties "went viral" worldwide, and people spoke. Countless thousands of e-mails, phone calls and written petitions bombarded politicians to pressure Sudan to release this innocent, Jesus-adoring woman and her two children.

The Lord demonstrated His gracious, sovereign power in response to this advocacy. He moved the hearts of presidents and kings. Governments took notice and began to reprimand the Sudanese government.

And today Meriam, Daniel and their children live and worship freely in the United States.

Mute No More includes, as part of our mission, the active advocacy for persecuted Christians around the world. We and several other of the organizations listed in Appendix B are exercising our voice toward this end and offer online advocacy tools to anyone willing to add their voices as well. We're providing information, guidance and technology to ensure that our concerned voices can be heard by authorities in our own country and around the world.

I've talked to many churches with international social justice and advocacy ministries for important causes, such as human trafficking. I didn't find one church that was pleading the cause of the afflicted saints. I suspect a few are out there somewhere, but I haven't found them. Every year, thousands of young teenage Christian girls in countries like Pakistan and Egypt are kidnapped, raped and forced to marry Muslim men, and then become slaves for the rest of their lives. Why aren't we speaking up for them and the countless other Christians who are unjustly imprisoned, tortured, beaten, enslaved and oppressed? Our muted brothers and sisters are like sheep being herded helplessly to slaughter.

We can make a difference! We must break our silence and show the proof of our love.

RELIEF AND DEVELOPMENT: REACH OUT YOUR HAND TO THE MUTE

Who then is the faithful and wise servant, whom the master has put in charge of the servants in his household to give them their food at the proper time? It will be good for that servant whose master finds him doing so when he returns. (Matthew 24:45–46)

Finally, the proof of our genuine love will be visible (or not) in our checkbook registers. Millions of persecuted believers around the world are in need of assistance from us, their brothers and sisters who have been entrusted with liberty and abundance. Many of us in the US have "the goods of this world" (1 John 3:17, NASB). We are therefore responsible to "share with God's people who are in need" by providing for their physical needs (Romans 12:13; see also James 2:16). In this day of globally available information we can all "see our brother in need," to adapt the words of John (1 John 3:17). Although we may not literally *see* the persecuted, we know about them, and John's instruction—and Jesus' new command—still holds us accountable for the information readily available to us concerning our spiritual family's suffering. Righteousness requires that awareness or access to information must lead to action.

Here are just a few of the ways we can help through financial support:

1. Providing for believers who have been forced to leave behind their homes, possessions and livelihoods, who are now dependent on the body of Christ for food, clothing and shelter.

2. Helping women and children in distress (James 1:27) because their husbands and fathers have been murdered or imprisoned for their faith. These incarcerated and murdered men are often church leaders, and they usually represent the only source of income for their already impoverished families.

3. Rescuing the millions of believers who are forced, expressly because of their faith, to live in literal garbage dumps and other putrid environments. They are denied access to housing, education and reasonable employment that would sustain their families.

4. Providing costly medical assistance for believers who have been tortured and beaten.

5. Providing legal assistance for Christians who have been unjustly treated, falsely accused and imprisoned. These believers are often already impoverished before their arrest, and in prison they're unable to work to support their families, let alone to pay legal fees.

Numerous organizations minister to the physical needs of suffering people around the world. Only a few organizations specialize in ministering to persecuted Christians. Don't assume that an organization's aid is targeted toward persecuted Christians; ask them.

Ministry to persecuted Christians is complex and dangerous work—dangerous for both the helping organization and for the recipients. This type of ministry usually must be conducted discreetly through trusted indigenous churches and partners who have the ability to deliver aid under the radar, undetected by watchful adversaries. Several of the organizations listed in Appendix B specialize in and have a proven ability to effectively provide aid to persecuted Christians. I encourage you to generously support these types of organizations Or you can send tax-deductible donations to Mute No More, where we commit to use 100 percent of all funds received to benefit the persecuted body of Christ. For additional information on this, go to *www.MuteNoMore.com/donations*

MAKE A STATEMENT

Signing the Heirloom Love Confession is a great way to help solidify your good intentions. The following sample is provided for you to review. I urge you to join the community of sincere believers who are signing the confession online at *www.MuteNoMore.com/confession*. Together, we're making a powerful and encouraging statement to each other and, perhaps more importantly, to our persecuted brothers and sisters about our unified agreement to remember them.

HEIRLOOM LOVE
CONFESSION

I understand that millions of Christians are being persecuted around the world.

I also understand that, since I am a follower of Jesus Christ, His new command requires me to love, remember and, as able, help suffering and persecuted fellow believers in the household of faith.

I confess that I have not loved and remembered my persecuted fellow believers in accordance with the teachings and requirements of Scripture.

I agree to change my ways and to sincerely seek to practice biblical love for Christians who are suffering and persecuted for their faith.

To sign, go to *www.MuteNoMore.com/confession.*

CHAPTER 15

Let Brotherly Love Continue

You may choose to look the other way but you can never say again that you did not know.

—William Wilberforce

If you saw a gang of thugs brutally beating Jesus, would you intervene? If you knew Jesus was living in a squalid refugee camp—or a garbage dump—because those who hate Him had destroyed His home, how much of your abundance would you give up to provide Him food, shelter, clothing and medical care? If Jesus was on death row, about to be wrongfully executed for blasphemy, would you speak out for Him? Would you and your church mourn and cry out in an all-night prayer vigil for His release?

What would you do for Jesus?

Our King speaks today: "I tell you the truth, whatever you did for one of the least of these brothers of mine, you did for me" (Matthew 25:40).

Jesus is here today. He lives in North Korea, Sudan, Syria, Eritrea, China, Laos, Vietnam, Burma, Pakistan, Iran, Nigeria and India, where He is suffering at the hands of those who loathe Him. Millions of Jesus' followers in dozens of countries are bearing His reproach today. They are falsely accused, imprisoned, beaten, tortured, raped, enslaved and murdered every day. Are you grieved? Fervent in prayer? Giving sacrificially? Speaking out on their behalf?

We demonstrate our love for Jesus by our acts of compassion for the persecuted saints. The opposite is also true: We reject Jesus by failing to care for His suffering children. "I tell you the truth, whatever you did not do for one of the least of these, you did not do for me" (Matthew 25:45).

Jesus said, "He who rejects you rejects me" (Luke 10:16). The Sudanese Muslims were persecuting Jesus when they killed more than two million Christians between 1984 and 2005. For two horror-filled decades their screams went up. And we, like acquiescent accomplices, forsook Jesus when we forsook the Sudanese Christians during this great tragedy.

Our sin of silence, and the genocide in Sudan, continue. We must repent and take action. Sudanese President al-Bashir—guilty of genocide in world opinion—continues in power and *still today* pursues the extinction of Christians in Sudan. As before, American Christians remain silent.

Many of us, when confronted with these facts and with our scriptural mandate, experience guilt feelings. This is good. Guilt is a signal that we're in need of grace and change. Praise the Lord for His gracious mercy, expressed through John's reminder: "If we confess our sins, he is faithful and just and will forgive us our sins and purify us from all unrighteousness" (1 John 1:9). Let us each, if appropriate, come before the throne of grace and find fresh forgiveness. Then let us go and practice sincere love toward our suffering siblings.

May heirloom love—the love that Jesus taught and is from above—be preserved in our hearts. May we never be satisfied with the flavorless "love" that is from the world. May heirloom love flow through us and inspire others to turn to authentic Christianity.

Let us love one another just as Jesus has loved us.

Rescue those being led away to death;
hold back those staggering toward slaughter.
If you say, "But we knew nothing about this,"
does not he who weighs the heart perceive it?
Does not he who guards your life know it?
Will he not repay each person according to what he has done?
(Proverbs 24:11–12)

New Testament References to Money and Giving

GENERAL TEACHING

Matthew 2:11; 5:42; 6:19–24; 13:7,22; 13:44–46; 14:20; 15:5–6; 17:27; 21:12–13

Mark 1:44; 4:7, 18–19; 6:42–43; 7:11–13; 11:15–17; 12:17; 12:41–44; 14:5–9

Luke 6:24–25; 6:30–36; 6:38; 8:7,14; 14:33; 19:11–27; 19:45–46; 20:21–26; 21:1–4

John 2:14–16; 12:3–8

1 Timothy 6:5–11; 6:17–19

2 Timothy 3:2

Hebrews 11:4; 13:5

James 1:9–11; 4:3–4

Revelation 3:14–22

POOR, SUFFERING AND PERSECUTED SAINTS[34]

Matthew 24:42–51; 25:1–46

Luke 12:13–48; 15:1–32; 16:1–31

Acts 2:44–45; 4:32–37; 5:1–10; 11:29–30

Romans: 12:8,13; 15:26–28

1 Corinthians 16:1–4

2 Corinthians 8:1–24; 9:1–15

Galatians 2:9–10; 6:7–10

2 Timothy 1:15–18

James 1:27; 2:1–26; 5:1–6

1 John 3:10–24

THE POOR IN GENERAL

Matthew 6:1–4; 19:16–26; 23:23–28

Mark 10:17–31

Luke 10:30–37; 11:37–42; 14:13–14; 18:18–30; 19:1–10; 3:7–11

Acts 10:1–4,31; 20:34–35

Ephesians 4:28

MISSIONARIES, GOSPEL TEACHERS AND LEADERS

Matthew 10:9–10

Luke 8:3; 10:7

Romans 1:13; 15:24; 16:1–2

1 Corinthians 9:1–17; 16:5–6,17

2 Corinthians 1:15–16; 11:7–9

Galatians 6:6

Philippians 2:29–30; 4:10–19

1 Thessalonians 5:12–13

2 Thessalonians 3:8–9

1 Timothy 5:17–18

2 Timothy 2:6

Titus 3:13

Philemon 1:7

1 Peter 5:2

3 John 1:5–8

Christian Persecution-Related Ministries

Disclaimer: This list is not comprehensive. My intent in providing this list is to offer a starting point, to save you some time and effort by identifying several organizations that I am aware of. I have limited or no experience with many of these ministries, and I am not endorsing them. I urge you to carefully evaluate the integrity, work and effectiveness of these ministries before supporting them.

21st Century Wilberforce Initiative

Barnabas Fund

China Aid

Christian Freedom International

Christian Post

Christian Broadcasting Network (CBN)

Christian Solidarity International

Christian Solidarity Worldwide

Christians in Crisis

Connecting Lives International Mission

Family Research Council

Global Response Network

Hardwired

Hudson Institute—Center for Religious Freedom

In Defense of Christians

International Christian Concern

International Christian Response

Institute on Religion and Democracy

Iraqi Christian Relief Council

Jubilee Campaign

Morning Star News

NK (North Korea) Missions

Nuba Reports

Open Doors

Philos Project

Religious Freedom Coalition

Religious Freedom Institute

Religious Liberty Partnership

Persecution Project Foundation

SHAI Fund

Voice of the Martyrs

Voice of the Persecuted

World Watch Monitor

Praying for the Persecuted Church

Intercede for our persecuted brothers and sisters, asking the Lord to help them do these things:

1. Pay close attention to the truth so they do not drift away from it (Hebrews 2:1).

2. Consider and emulate Jesus, the Apostle and High Priest of their confession, who was faithful to Him who appointed Him (3:1–2).

3. Hold fast until the end their confidence and the hope in which they boast (3:6).

4. Take care to avoid an evil, unbelieving heart that falls away from the living God (3:12).

5. Encourage one another day after day, as long as it is still called "Today," so that none of them will be hardened by the deceitfulness of sin (3:13).

6. Hold firmly till the end the confidence they had at first (3:14).

7. Keep their hearts from hardening (4:7).

8. Hold fast their confession that Jesus is Lord (4:14).

9. Draw near with confidence to the throne of grace where they receive mercy and find grace to help in time of need (4:16).

10. Imitate those who through faith and patience inherit the promises (6:12).

11. Have strong encouragement to take hold of the hope set before them (6:18).

12. Draw near to the Lord with a sincere heart in full assurance of faith (10:22).

13. Hold fast the confession of their hope without wavering, remembering that He who promised is faithful (10:23).

14. Consider how to stimulate one another to love and good deeds (10:24).

15. Have courage so as to not forsake assembling together, but that they would encourage one another; and all the more as they see the day drawing near (10:25).

16. Not throw away their confidence, which has a great reward (10:35).

17. Have endurance, so that when they have done the will of God, they may receive what was promised (10:36).

18. Have faith to the preserving of the soul, rather than shrink back to destruction (10:39).

19. Lay aside every encumbrance and the sin which so easily entangles, and run with endurance the race set before them (12:1).

20. Fix their eyes on Jesus, the author and perfecter of faith, who for the joy set before Him endured the cross, despising the shame, and has sat down at the right hand of the throne of God (12:2).

21. Consider Him who has endured such hostility by sinners against Himself, so that they will not grow weary and lose heart (12:3).

22. Strengthen the hands that are weak and the knees that are feeble (12:12).

23. Make straight paths for their feet, so that the limb which is lame may not be put out of joint, but rather be healed (12:13).

24. Pursue peace with all men, and the sanctification without which no one will see the Lord (12:14).

25. Not come short of the grace of God or allow any root of bitterness to spring up and cause trouble, defiling many (12:15).

26. Be blameless and innocent, children of God above reproach in the midst of a crooked and perverse generation, among whom they appear as lights in the world (Philippians 2:15).

27. Find strength and protection from the evil one, and to be rescued from perverse and evil men (2 Thessalonians 3:1–3).

28. Not worry about how or what they're to speak, but believe that the Spirit of their Father will give them the words when they need them (Matthew 10:19–20).

29. Not fear those who kill the body but are unable to kill the soul, but rather fear Him who is able to destroy both soul and body in hell (10:28).

30. Remember that no sparrow falls to the ground apart from their Father's will, and that they're worth more than many sparrows (10:29–31).

Notes

1 Some of these verses do not specifically indicate why the Christians in these passages were suffering or in need. However, because persecution is almost continuously an understood part of the New Testament context, these Scriptures likely refer to Christians who were suffering and in need due to persecution. Biblical references to "the poor" and "the needy" refer to people who are suffering and perishing because they do not have daily food or other basic resources necessary to sustain life (see, for example, Luke 3:11; James 2:15–16).

2 See "2014 Annual Report," United States Commission on International Religious Freedom, 2014, accessible via uscirf.gov/reports-briefs/annual-report/2014-annual-report.

3 Sur's perceptions of events are fictionalized, but he and the events portrayed are completely real.

4 Information for this story was compiled from dozens of reports accessible through World Watch Monitor at worldwatchmonitor.org; Human Rights Watch for Lao Religious Freedom at hrwlrf.net; Mission Network News at mnnonline.org (all accessed during AprilJune 2013, search terms: *katin laos* via each site's search engine); and from private letters from unidentifiable sources in country.

5 Carl Moeller, "Millions Are Persecuted, and the Church Wants to Know," ChristianHeadlines.com, October 21, 2011, christianheadlines.com/news/millions-persecuted-church-wants-to-know.html.

6 See Acts 2:41,47; 4:4; 5:14; 6:1,7.

7 See Romans 15:25–26; 1 Corinthians 16:1; 2 Corinthians 8:1–5.

8   Hebrews 11:13–16: "All these people were still living by faith when
    they died. They did not receive the things promised; they only saw
    them and welcomed them from a distance, admitting that they
    were foreigners and strangers on earth. People who say such things
    show that they are looking for a country of their own. If they
    had been thinking of the country they had left, they would have
    had opportunity to return. Instead, they were longing for a better
    country—a heavenly one. Therefore God is not ashamed to be called
    their God, for he has prepared a city for them."

9   See Isaiah 53:7.

10 Sources: Helen Berhane, *Song of the Nightingale* (London: Authentic
    Media, 2009); "CSW Month of Campaigning for Eritrea Culminates
    in Launch of Gospel Album," Christian Solidarity Worldwide, June 2,
    2006, csw.org.uk/2006/06/02/press/517/article.htm; "Eritrean Gospel
    Singer Helen Berhane Released from Prison," Christian Solidarity
    Worldwide, November 3, 2006, csw.org.uk/2006/11/03/press/569/
    article.htm; now-unavailable report, Assist News, accessed April 23,
    2013, assistnews.net/stories/2013/s13040060.htm.

11 According to the president of the Pakistan Christian Congress.

12 Sources: "Pakistan: A 12-Year-Old Christian Is Gang-Raped for Eight
    Months, Forcibly Converted and Then 'Married' to Her Muslim
    Attacker," Asian Human Rights Commission, October 10, 2011,
    humanrights.asia/news/urgent-appeals/AHRC-UAC-199–2011;
    Ali Usman, "Cash for Kidneys: Pakistan's Flourishing Trade in
    Illegal Transplants," *Express Tribune*, July 23, 2012, tribune.com.pk/
    story/411570/cash-for-kidneys-pakistans-flourishing-trade-in-illegal-
    transplants.

13 Selected sources: "Shin Dong-hyuk," *Wikipedia*, last modified on
    February 10, 2016, en.wikipedia.org/wiki/Shin_Dong-hyuk; Blaine
    Harden, *Escape from Camp 14* (New York: Penguin, 2012), as excerpted
    in "How One Man Escaped from a North Korean Prison Camp,"

Guardian, accessed April 11, 2013, webcitation.org/66Wl65MSi; "Thank You, Father Kim Il Sung," transcript of November 15, 2005, hearing by United States Commission on International Religious Freedom, uscirf. gov/sites/default/files/resources/stories/pdf/nkstudypressconf.pdf; David Hawk, "Thank You, Father Kim Il Sung," United States Commission on International Religious Freedom, November 2005, uscirf.gov/sites/ default/files/resources/stories/pdf/nkwitnesses_wgraphics.pdf (the story of the twenty-five church members is on pages 51–52).

14 You can watch the video, "A Hidden Hunger: Life in the Caves of the Nuba Mountains," Nuba Reports, November 20, 2012, nubareports. org/a-hidden-hunger-life-in-the-caves-of-the-nuba-mountains.

15 Sources: Hundreds of reports and videos at NubaReports.org; Eric Reeves, "Compromising with Evil: An Archival History of Greater Sudan, 2007–2012," dedicated report website, originally released October 22, 2012, last revised January 1, 2013, complete report accessible and downloadable from CompromisingWithEvil.org.

16 Sources: Nuri Kino, "Between the Barbed Wire," January 11, 2013, aina.org/reports/bbw.pdf; "Syrian Civil War," *Wikipedia,* last updated on April 3, 2016, en.wikipedia.org/wiki/Syrian_Civil_War; USCIRF Special Report: "Protecting and Promoting Religious Freedom in Syria," April 2013, uscirf.gov/sites/default/files/resources/Syria%20 Report%20April%202013(1).pdf; CNN Library, "Syria Civil War Fast Facts," World Vision staff, "Syria Refugee Crisis FAQ: How the War Is Affecting Children," World Vision, May 11, 2016, worldvision.org/wv/ news/Syria-war-refugee-crisis-FAQ; "Quick Facts: What You Need to Know About the Syria Crisis," Mercy Corps, updated March 1, 2016, mercycorps.org/articles/iraq-jordan-lebanon-syria-turkey/quick-facts-what-you-need-know-about-syria-crisis.

17 The three "selfs" refer to self-governance, self-support and self-propagation and were first devised in the mid-twentieth century by biblically sound Christian leaders to discourage reliance on foreign

influence, rightly encouraging Chinese leadership for the Chinese churches. The "selfs" principles appealed to the Chinese government, which appropriated the terminology for its own sanctioned version of Christianity with no "meddling" from Western influence. Notice that this Communist Party-run organization is purposefully termed a "movement," not a church. And it is "patriotic," implying loyalty to China—specifically, to the Chinese Communist Party.

18 See Acts 17:10–11. Sources: Dozens of reports from ChinaAid.org; "Three Self Church," BillionBibles.org, page copyright date 2013, accessed April 3, 2016, billionbibles.org/china/three-self-church.html; Alcorn, Randy, several articles on the Eternal Perspective Ministries website, EPM.org; the Three Self Patriotic Movement's official website: bibleinchina.org.

19 See Leviticus 27:30,32; Numbers 18:24,28; Deuteronomy 12:11–12; 14:28–29.

20 Ravi Zacharias wrote these words in his afterword to Nina Shea, *In the Lion's Den* (Nashville: Broadman Holman, 1997).

21 Kirsten Powers, "A Global Slaughter of Christians, but America's Churches Stay Silent," The Daily Beast, September 27, 2013, thedailybeast.com/articles/2013/09/27/a-global-slaughter-of-christians-but-america-s-churches-stay-silent.html.

22 Interview of Wilfred Wong by Kim A. Lawton, Prague, Czech Republic, May 6, 1996.

23 First Peter 8:12, KJV; Acts 8:1.

24 Although the official name of this Southeast Asian country is now Myanmar, we'll use the older, familiar and still commonly used name, Burma.

25 Sources: Rajni George, "Life in Limbo for Chin Refugees," *New York Time*, November 30, 2011, india.blogs.nytimes.com/2011/11/30/life-in-

limbo-for-chin-refugees; Michelle A. Vu, "Illegal Aliens or Refugees? 100,000 Burmese Chin Christians in India," *Christian Post*, March 6, 2012, christianpost.com/news/illegal-aliens-or-refugees-100000-burmese-chin-christians-in-india-70954/#TYjdApjlTetwBRMr.99; Trent Franks, "Franks Statement on Human Rights in Burma" (speech presented in Tom Lantos Human Rights Commission hearing February 28, 2013), US Congressman Trent Franks's official website, franks.house.gov/franks-statement-human-rights-burma; Brendan Giusti, "Burma Christian Persecution: At Least 10 Killed in Grenade Attack on Orphanage," *Christian Post*, November 14, 2011, christianpost.com/news/burma-christian-persecution-at-least-10-killed-in-grenade-attack-on-orphange-61673.

26 Quoted in Dr. Dobson's April 1997 newsletter.

27 Ravi Zacharias wrote these words in his afterword to Nina Shea, *In the Lion's Den* (Nashville: Broadman Holman, 1997).

28 Some aspects of Namrata's perceptions of events are fictionalized, but she and the events portrayed are completely real.

29 Sources: Nirmala Carvalho, "Orissa: Christmas of Namrata, the Little Dalit Disfigured by a Bomb," AsiaNews.it, December 15, 2008, asianews.it/index.php?l=en&art=14009&size=A; Teresa Neumann, "Christian Girl, Disfigured by Bomb, Forgives Terrorists," Breaking Christian News, December 20, 2008, breakingchristiannews.com/articles/display_art.html?ID=6162; "Será Possível Esquecer?" Voz da Verdade (Voice of Truth), November 4, 2012, vozdaverdade.org/site/index.php?id=2918&cont_=ver2; Elizabeth Scalia, "'They Do Not Love Jesus,'" Patheos: Catholic Channel: The Anchoress, December 18, 2008, patheos.com/blogs/theanchoress/2008/12/18/they-do-not-love-jesus.

30 Sources: Hundreds of reports from OpenDoorsUSA.org and Persecution.org.

31 A published challenge from The Christian Association of Nigerian-Americans.

32 Mama Maggie Gobran led a comfortable life in Cairo as a Christian from a prominent Egyptian family before following a conviction from God to serve the poorest-of-the-poor Christian children and families who, due to persecution and oppression, have been forced to live in an active landfill—often referred to as "Garbage City."

33 Frank Wolf, "Obama Administration Needs to 'Find Its Voice' on Human Rights," The Hill, July 26, 2010, thehill.com/blogs/congress-blog/foreign-policy/110849-obama-administration-needs-to-find-its-voice-on-human-rights-rep-frank-wolf.

34 Matthew 24:42–51; 25:1–46; and Luke 12:13–48 contain Jesus' teachings on money and judgment. Jesus directed these teachings toward those of us who have been entrusted with money and other resources (Matthew 24:45; Luke 12:41–42). In summary, He taught that those who have been so entrusted are responsible and accountable for feeding and caring for needy saints, whom He referred to as "the least of these" (Matthew 25:31–46).

Luke 15:1–32 and 16:1–31 contain Jesus' teachings on repentance from squandering money. Here Jesus teaches us how to use money correctly by caring for the least of the saints, such as Lazarus. The emphasis in this sermon is on repentance from selfish consumption (Luke 16:19) and on helping suffering saints (16:9) without specific reference to the cause of their suffering.

In my book *Prodigal's Progress: From Loving Money to Loving God* I present an in-depth consideration of these Scripture passages.

Journal

CHAPTER 1

CHAPTER 2

It's human nature to resist change in ourselves, to resist admitting the need to think differently. Which mental or emotional barriers might you need to confront as you continue this journey? Take a moment to express to the Lord your openness to following His path, wherever He might take you.

CHAPTER 3

Previously, when you've read the New Testament's instructions about hospitality, to whom have you thought to apply them? Now that you know they were first intended to benefit persecuted Christian refugees, how does that affect your thinking and plans about how you will obey them?

CHAPTER 4

When eternity is on the line, it can't hurt to stop and ask yourself, "Have I really got it right? Do I understand how to be saved?"

If you have any doubt, prayerfully reread the Scriptures quoted in this chapter. Are you depending solely on the payment of Jesus' life for your forgiveness—as the Bible teaches—or are you depending on yourself or anything else?

CHAPTER 5

Write your own paraphrase of Jesus' command: "Love one another. As I have loved you, so you must love one another." Clarify what He meant by each component of the command.

CHAPTER 6

Picture Jesus standing before you in the flesh, destitute, starving, thirsty and mistreated. What are you willing to do for Him?

CHAPTER 7

In eternity, when you meet the Macedonian family—the parents, the children—who gave up regular meals in order to help brothers and sisters suffering in Judea, will you tell them how their examples prodded you toward sacrificial generosity to believers in Laos, Eritrea, Pakistan, or other places of oppression? Or will you lower your eyes in shame, knowing they gave out of their poverty and you held onto your abundance?

CHAPTER 8

Take a few minutes and meditate on 1 Peter 4:8. How does Peter's emphasis on loving needy fellow believers "above all" compare with your current priorities?

- *Honestly, how do you respond when you read John's black-and-white statements about who does and does not belong to Christ? Are they prompting you to change something in your relationship with the Lord or in how you use your time, energy, money and possessions?*

- *Why might Christians resist placing a biblical emphasis and priority on helping persecuted believers in Jesus? For each reason you think of, how would James (or other New Testament writers) respond?*

CHAPTER 9

Try applying the sincerity test to a spending decision you're facing. Which of your possible choices involves love that is . . .

- *Open and honest, rather than hiding?*
- *Pure and true, rather than polluted?*

CHAPTER 10

Carefully reread John 13:34; 15:12–14; Romans 12:1; and 1 John 3:16–18. Keep in mind the original context and intended meaning when John and Paul wrote these words. Picture also the faces of our brothers and sisters whose stories you've been reading throughout this book. Then consider: How much of your income and other resources is the Lord calling you to contribute toward the needs of the persecuted in Christ? How much does the test of sincere love allow you to consume or keep?

CHAPTER 11

CHAPTER 12

CHAPTER 13

When you learn about the horrible suffering of your spiritual family, you may take Nehemiah's words as a question for yourself: "How can I not be sad?" Take a few minutes and conduct an honest heart check. Our emotions—our joy and our sadness—are often a reflection of what we treasure. We mourn for the loss of whatever genuinely matters to us. As we learn to delight in the Lord's "majestic ones" (see Psalm 16:3, above), we'll naturally cultivate a heart of compassion that grieves for their suffering.

What makes you weep?

CHAPTER 14

CHAPTER 15